John Jardine

Notes on Buddhist Law

John Jardine

Notes on Buddhist Law

ISBN/EAN: 9783743315204

Manufactured in Europe, USA, Canada, Australia, Japa

Cover: Foto ©Lupo / pixelio.de

Manufactured and distributed by brebook publishing software
(www.brebook.com)

John Jardine

Notes on Buddhist Law

NOTES ON BUDDHIST LAW

BY THE JUDICIAL COMMISSIONER, BRITISH BURMA.

V.—INHERITANCE AND PARTITION.

PREFACE.

1. Translation by Mr. S. Minus of the Chapter on Inheritance and some miscellaneous sections of the Manoo Wonnana Dhammathat as edited in Burmese by Moung Tet Too, with Notes by J. Jardine, Esq., Judicial Commissioner of British Burma.

2. Translation of the Law of Inheritance according to the Wagaru Dhammathat by Dr. E. Forchhammer, Professor of Pali, from a Pali Manuscript on Palm Leaves in his possession.

RANGOON : PRINTED AT THE GOVERNMENT PRESS, 1883.

[Price—Re. 1·0·0.]

CONTENTS.

CHAPTER I.

ON THE DIVISION OF INHERITED PROPERTY.

ii.

CONTENTS.

CHAPTER II.

THE LAW REGARDING SONS.

CHAPTER V.

MISCELLANEOUS.

V.—INHERITANCE AND PARTITION.

By John Jardine, Esq., Bo. C.S., Judicial Commissioner of British Burma.

PREFACE.

It is a very singular fact that only one translation of any of the Burmese codified laws of inheritance has ever yet been made. Of course I allude to Dr. Richardson's *Menu Kyay*. As it is 60 years since the first British occupation, the rate of progress is only three translations in a century; and for this reason and to end the present state of things I have hurried through the Press a translation of the *Manoo Wonnana* Dhammathat on this part of the law.

2. The *Wonnana* was compiled by Kyaw Deng about 1772 from older sources. This was in the reign of Tsheng-bhoosheng, the son of Alompra. The book is extremely valued by the Burmese as a recent and authoritative statement of their law and ought to be interesting to Europeans as a great and successful attempt at written codification. The English conquerors have up till now been puzzled to know what to do with these complete and very modern codes; they were ignorant of any key to the origin and interpretation; and under these circumstances it is not to be wondered at that a need was soon felt and a desire expressed for a code within a code, a compendium which would state rules in a way comprehensible to the English and would cut difficult points by legislative decisions. The theory used as a lever to get this done is stated by Major Sparks in 1860; it was assumed that side by side with the written codes of 1768, 1770, and 1772 there were inconsistent local customs and "an unwritten code engraved in the minds of the people.". Major Sparks' code was to combine the written law with the local custom, the assumption being that the recent Burmese codifiers had dealt only with written law and ignored custom altogether.

3. I have never seen any evidence to justify the assumption that the Burman Emperors and their chancellors were guilty of such folly and want of statesmanship; but it has been the fashion of English writers to charge them with inconsistency, contradictions, and puerilities ever since. The other assumption that there is a body of unwritten law not based on

these codes, but entitled to recognition as established customs, is not based on any evidence that I know of or supported by judicial decision ; it is, I suspect, a purely English idea and is hardly hinted at by the Natives in the correspondence about the printing of Dhammathats in 1872 or in that about wills in 1882. A perusal of these replies shows the reader that almost every writer treats the Dhammathats as the only source of Native law, and that the people award these codes a religious veneration because of their supposed conformity or connection with the Buddhist faith. Of course I except from these remarks the wild tribes of the mountains and such peoples as the Shans and Karens, who have customs of their own.

4. I have never been able to understand the reasoning which insists that the codes which the Burman Emperors had promulgated not long before our first conquests were not the statute law of the country at the time. If, for example, as most of them do, they contain the ancient Indian recognition of primogeniture, it is perhaps too much to say that the right of primogeniture was never law here, because it is abrogated in India, or because the people dispose of successions by special contracts of their own. Before we infer a general custom having the force of law, we should at least find out whether the instances are not the result of special contracts and compromises ("Bhau Nanaji *vs.* Sundrabai," 11 Bombay H. C. R. 249). Major Sparks ignores the eldest son's right to a special share ; but Burmans, aware of their own codified law, say that the right exists under their codes, although seldom exacted by the eldest son.

5. The correspondence about wills and gifts shows, as do the judgments on inheritance and divorce, the most violent differences of opinion among Burman lawyers and elders as to what the law is and what it ought to be. The Courts not having recognized that the greater part of the written law is borrowed from India, have for years left the most important subjects unsettled. Even, if as has been suggested by high authority, a new code should be made out of the Burmese codes, the work would be unsafe if undertaken without a competent knowledge of the latter, and there would be a danger of the code being drafted in terms better suited to the English intellect than to the language and ideas of the people. At present every little Judge is a law to himself and settles questions about divorce and inheritance in his own way, and his decisions become law to the people around. Occasionally a judgment is appealed and argued and a binding precedent

made by the highest Court.   Whether the expensive piece-
meal legislation of the Judges, or the direct settlement by the
Legislature, will terminate the existing uncertainties is a
matter of opinion : in either case a second translation of a code
will be valuable.   I have indicated some of the Indian sources
of the law and the constructions of the Hindu sages as well
as decisions of the Courts.   But no translation is sufficient
unless it gives accurate account of Pali terms of law and
shows from the Indian source whether by *property* or *inheritance* ancestral property alone is meant and so on.

6.   I may here express a hope that this translation may be
some help to scholars in settling the date of the Indian codes
used by the Burmans as law ; but until much progress has
been made and some theory ascertained as to whether they
were imported in Sanscrit or Pali, more than this would be in-
appropriate.   If I may again urge the subject, I would entreat
the members of the service to which Colebrooke belonged to
do their part in learned investigation.   Professor Max Müller
lately impressed on the new Civil Service the need of exertion
to keep up with the traditions of the past and the regard for
Oriental literature which distinguished so many of the civilians
in former days.   So far as I know, the learned discoveries made
in Burma have been effected by the military civilians, and I
do not see why such examples should be neglected.

7.   I here express my thanks to Dr. Forchhammer for the
translation of ss. 63 and 74 to 80 inclusive and 102: they
presented difficulties to ordinary translators.

RANGOON :

15th March 1883.

JOHN JARDINE,

Judicial Commissioner.

Translation by Mr. S. Minus of the Chapter on Inheritance and some miscellaneous sections of the Manoo Wonnana Dhammathat as edited in Burmese by Moung Tet Too, with Notes by J. Jardine, Esq., Judicial Commissioner of British Burma.

THE following are the seven kinds of claims to the estate of mother and father :—

(1) the claim made by sons from the mother ;
(2) the claim made by daughters from the mother ;
(3) the claim made by daughters from the father ;
(4) the claim made by sons from the father ;
(5) the claim made by one son from the other of the same mother and father (own brothers) ;
(6) the claim made by daughters and sons of the lower wife from the daughters and sons of the higher (great) wife ;
(7) the claim made by daughters and sons of the (greater) first husband from the daughters and sons of the second husband.

Note.—These claims are discussed in the above order in s. 10 and following sections.

S. 2. The following is the mode of division when a man has a wife of the noble (*min*) class, a wife of the Brahmin class, a wife of the trading class, and a wife of the cultivating class. If the husband of these wives dies, the property should be divided into ten parts, and four parts be given to the wife of the noble (*min*) class, three parts to the wife of the Brahmin class, two parts to the wife of the trading class, and one part to the wife of the cultivating class. In this way the division should be made proportionally according to the class. If there be two wives of the noble (*min*) class and only three women of the remaining classes, let the property be divided into 14 parts and distributed as above shown. If there be three women, one of each of the other classes, let the property be divided into six parts, and, as above stated, let it be distributed in the proportion of three, two, and one.

If there are two wives, one of superior and the other of inferior class, and if the one of superior class has no sons or daughters and the inferior only has, let the husband's estate be equally divided between them. Other classes of wives besides these abovementioned, in other words, wives who live in separate houses from the wife who eats together *with the husband*, should only get the things which were given to them, and should not get things not in their possession.

Although this is laid down, if the husband with the wife or the wife with the husband eat and drink and the (pahyin) property originally brought becomes exhausted, no damage shall be given.

S. 3.   If *a man* has the following six kinds of wives, namely,—

a wife of the noble (min) class ;
a wife of the military commander (sit-thoogyee) class ;
a wife of the wealthy (thootay) class ;
a wife of the Brahmin class ;
a wife of the trading class ; and
a wife of the poor class ;

the wife of the noble class and the wife of the warrior class shall *each* receive five parts ; the wife of the wealthy class four parts ; the wife of the Brahmin class three parts ; the wife of the trading class two parts ; and the wife of the poor class one part.   If they have children, the property shall be divided in the same proportion as laid down for their parents.

S. 4.   If a Brahmin has a wife of the Brahmin class, a wife of the noble class, a wife of the trading class, and a wife of the poor class, the wife of the Brahmin class shall receive four parts, the wife of the noble (*min*) class three parts, the wife of the trading class two parts, and the wife of the ploughing class one part only.

Note.—The legal relations of wives of different classes are left untouched by Major Sparks in his Code, probably because such distinctions are obsolete among the Burman Buddhists of the present time.   The rules bear traces of Brahmanical ideas; and it seems there once was a time when the higher classes of Burmans and Brahmans had a position relatively superior to the others than what they occupy now.   Captain Forbes, at page 24 of his book on the " Languages of Further India," quotes the traveller Fitch on this subject : " Fitch had evidently an idea that Pegu " was then occupied by two distinct races, for he says,—' The Bramas which be of the " king's country (for the king is a Brama) have their legs or bellies, or some part of " their body, made black with certain things which they have, they use to prick the " skin. * * * And this is accounted an honour among them, but none may have it " but the Bramas which are of the king's kindred.'   " This," says Captain Forbes, " exactly describes the case.   Tattooing is a Burman and not a Mon-Anam custom. " The ancient Talaings or Mons never tattooed their bodies, and the moderns have " learnt the custom from the Burmans."

The Dhammathats also deal in considerable detail with wives of different classes.   As in the old Hindu law, priority was decided by order of class (Sir Thomas Strange's Hindu law 56), but the present rule is that of priority of marriage (s. 37 of Bk. 10 of the *Menu Kyay*), where the wives are of the same class as now among Hindus (8 Madras H.C.R. 424), at least if the senior wife is living with her husband ; but in s. 38 of Bk. 10 of the *Menu Kyay* the criterion is the number of male children.   For the case of a Brahman grahasta or householder see s. 4 of Bk. 11 of the *Menu Kyay*.   Ss. 47 and 48 of Bk. 3 apply to debts the same principle as the sections under comment apply to assets.   This part of the subject is discussed in my first Notes on Buddhist law.   The social equality implied in the husband allowing his partner to eat out of the same dish appears to have been considered one criterion of her being a wife and as such having the rights to maintenance and inheritance and inconsistent with any lower status. Several such wives might live in separate houses and yet each eat out of the same dish with the husband.   In s. 33 below we see that the same principle of partition was applied to the children of wives of different classes.

In sections 2, 3, and 4 of the *Wonnana* no mention is made of children, but the proportions of division among wives of different classes are the same as are found for sons of wives of different caste by some of the Hindu lawyers, Vishnu, Manu, and Yajnawalkya (Colebrooke V. Dig. 139, 140, 142, 153), in cases at least where no deduction was made for the eldest son in recognition of primogeniture.

Manu.—Or, if no deduction be made, let some person learned in the law divide the whole collected estate into ten parts and make a legal distribution by the following rule :—Let the son of the Brahmani take four parts, the son of the Kshatriya, three ; let the son of the Vaisya have two parts ; let the son of the Sudra take a single part if he be virtuous.

The principle of the division into 14 shares in section 2 is based by Colebrooke on this text. Where no deduction was made for the eldest son, the proportions given by Manu are 3, 2, 1½, and 1. Two questions arise for scholars to investigate, *viz.,* why does this Burmese law make no mention of sons but treat the widows as heirs ; and how and when did the division of people into six classes arise ? The following observations by Professor Sarvadhikari (Tagore Law Lectures, 1880, page 239) on the institutes of Gautama, which, according to Max Müller, belong to a period contemporary with the first spreading of Buddhism in India, are useful as explaining some of the inconsistencies of the Hindu law :—

" At the time when Gautama was promulgating his rules of inheritance a great, evil, which is insuperable from a polygamous state of society, had become manifest. As soon as the old restraints were loosened, as soon as the family ceased to hold together and the individual members freed themselves from the salutary subjection of the patriarch, the evils of polygamy showed themselves. All the wives of the husband strove to secure his property for their own issue. The rule of primogeniture would have continued in full force for a very long time in India had polygamy not existed in the country. Polygamy is adverse to the rule of hereditary succession. It requires no explanation to make it clear to you that in polygamous societies the form of primogeniture will always tend to vary."

The fear of capricious division of property in a society where polygamy exists and where, if the Extra Assistant Commissioner of Toungoop is right, few couples are married for life, was given as a reason by several persons consulted against the conferring of a power to make wills in 1882.

For further discussion of *anuloma* marriages and the Hindu authorities, see Tagore Law Lectures, 1879, page 150, where the meaning of *patni,* or lawful wife, is considered. The rule dividing an estate according to the number of mothers rather than sons is as old as Gautama and Haradatta (*see* Colebrooke, V. Dig. 59 to 63, and Bühler's Gautama, 28, 17), but in early times applied only where the mothers were of equal class. As to the *dasi* whom the *Smriti Chandrika* treats as a slave wife in opposition to the *patni* or *agnihotrin, see* the judgment of the Bombay High Court in " Rahi *vs.* Govind "(I. L. R. 1 Bombay, 98). The opposition between lawful wife and slave wife appears from the plaints in the appendix to III Notes on Buddhist law to be commonly known to the Burmans at the present day.

S. 5. If there are the awratha, khettaza, and the hettima sons, the awratha son shall receive four parts, the hettima son one part, and the khettaza son only half of one part. Although it is said that he shall receive half of one part, if his mother is living that portion shall go to her. It is only when the mother is not living that the khettaza son gets the half of one part.

Note.—These three kinds of children are defined and classified among the six children entitled to inherit in the discussion after ss. 81, Bk. 10, of the *Menu Kyay.* See also ss. 81 and 84 below.

S. 6. If relative slaves have large amount of property, and if they and their relative slaves die, two portions of the estate of the deceased slaves shall be given to their wives and sons (children) and one portion to their master's living relations.

S. 7. If an awratha son and a kittima son *both* live in the house of the mother and father, the awratha son shall receive five parts and the kittima son only one part. If the awratha son lives in a separate house, he shall only get four parts. If the kittima son lives in a separate house, he is not entitled to the inheritance property of the mother and father.

Note.—Sandford J. ruled the following on the *Menu Kyay*, Bk. 10, ss. 25 and 26, and evidence of custom ("Nga Meng Gyaw *vs.* Me Pee," Sandford's Rulings 4): "An adopted child, by marrying and living separately from his adoptive "parents, does not, by the mere fact of marriage, forfeit his rights of inheritance "in this adoptive family. But the burden of proving that he has performed the "duties necessary to be performed by an adopted child will be thrown upon him, "and, in the absence of such proof, the Courts will disallow his claim to inherit. "Mere occasional assist ance on the part of the adopted child is not sufficient to "preserve his rights of inheritance."

As to evidence of adoption, its essentials, and the right of an adopted son or daughter to inherit, see "Ma Goon *vs.* Ma Goon" (Sandford's Rulings, 22 and 30).

In these cases no allusion is made to the Hindu law; and I know of no decision on the points as to who may adopt, who may give in adoption, or who may be adopted, matters of great importance in the law of husband and wife. The case in the *Menu Kyay*, Bk. 6, s. 30, of a person without relations attaching himself to some one who thus adopts him was also left unnoticed.

S. 8. If there are no awratha and kittima sons, the apatitha son and *his own brothers*, the son of the same parents, shall receive equal *shares*. Only when there are no sons, as abovementioned, who are heirs shall *the property* go to Government (mins) (ဝင်းတိုက်သက္ကော).

Note.—The apatitha son is not mentioned in the *Menu Kyay* or defined in the *Wonnana*. In the *Smriti Chandrika* the apavidha son is defined as one whom a man receives as his own after desertion by both or either of the son's parents.

As to escheat to Government among Hindus, *see* 8 Moore's Indian Appeals, 500.

S. 9. If there be many slaves and property which should be called inheritance, they shall not be divided during the lifetime of the father and mother, *i.e.*, two individuals.

Note.—As to the wife's rights to property during marriage, *see* my Notes on Buddhist law—I. Marriage : its incidents. As to the rights of the widow on the death of the father and the claim of children to partition, *see* "Mee Loung *vs.* Mee Koon" in an appendix to Note III and the authorities there quoted out of other Dhammathats. For the discussion of the widow's rights at Hindu law, *see* Colebrooke's Digest, Bk. 5, ch. 8, text 115, *Vrihaspati*. On failure of both their parents, partition among brothers is ordained.

Consequently, it is argued that, "after the death of the father two periods occur for partition, when the mother dies, or, while living, when she consents." This view of some of the Hindu lawyers is distinctly adopted in the *Menu Kyay*, Bk. 10, ss. 11 and 12, for which *see* my Note to s. 12 below. There is a full discussion in the *Smriti Chandrika*.

S. 10. There are seven ways of demanding inheritance from the father and mother as mentioned in the beginning, and of these seven ways the following shall be considered as the rule of inheritance between the mother and sons. After the father's death, if the son bears the father's responsibility, such eldest son gets the lance used by the father, and also all such articles of use, and elephant, betel-box, teapot, cups used in betel-boxes, sword-bearer, umbrella-holder, and other followers, being animate and inanimate things always used (by the father). He shall also, in the first instance, get the riding horse and ass and also the vegetable garden, paddy land, house and land separately. No son shall forcibly take the waistband, earrings, hairpin, bracelets, ring, &c., palanquin, cymbals, as are given to wear and use during the father's lifetime. Of the bullocks, buffaloes, goats, pigs, and paddy land, being property other than those described above, the mother shall get three shares and the son one share. Beside these the remaining inanimate property, namely, gold and silver, shall be divided in the same manner. The son was unable to give any assistance at the time the property was acquired, and the father did not take care of the property that was acquired, and for this reason the mother is entitled to get three shares, and if the son takes his father's place he gets one share. As the mother had been looking after and feeding them she shall get three of the male slaves and the son one. The mother shall get all the female slaves. Even if there be ten sons, it shall be the same. If there be female slaves, only the mother shall divide them and give an appropriate number to the son. This relates only to "letthetpwa" property and slaves. If there be any slaves brought by the father, they shall be divided equally with the mother. The division between the daughter and father, as far as it relates to slaves, shall be the same as this.

Note.—The peculiar portion of the eldest son is defined in similar terms in the *Menu Kyay*, ss. 5 and 11. Many of the articles are emblems of rank and some are impartible. The reader will observe the proximity of the text to those about wives of different classes. The Hindu text most resembling the catalogue of the *Wonnana* is that which defines the peculiar share of the son of the Brahmana wife (Colebrooke V. Dig. 139).

Manu.—The chief servant in husbandry, the bull kept for impregnating cows, the riding horse or carriage, the ring and other ornaments, and the principal messuage shall be deducted from the inheritance and given to the Brahmana son, together with a larger share by way of pre-eminence.

Colebrooke explains that the rule relates also to partition among the sons of one mother; and desert, learning, and virtue were also causes of pre-eminence. Whether the right of the eldest son to the peculiar articles, or, on partition among brethren, to a larger share than the rest are now generally admitted in Burman families, I have no sufficient means of knowing; it seems that the corresponding duty at Hindu law is one of piety only, and that the younger children are not under the ordinary law of descent obliged to give the eldest son any pecuniary recognition of his pre-eminence (Colebrooke V. Dig. 61).

For some historical account of the decay of the ideas of primogeniture from the time of Gautama downwards and the rise of the doctrine of equal distribution, the reader may consult the Tagore Law Lectures, 1880, where the rules of the Hindu writers are collected at page 231 and their various characters accounted for.

As to the Hindu interpretation of the eldest son's right to the family house and the saving of the rights of the rest, *see* Colebrooke V. Dig. 46.

Harita avoids giving the eldest son a right to turn out all the others from the family abode. Therefore does the sage add: Let them remove and erect habitations beyond the limits of the court or yard; but if they cannot remove and erect other houses, then the best apartment shall be assigned to the eldest. Chandeswara so expounds the text. A young Burman judge of the present day, ignorant of the origin of the text and of these ancient interpretations, would probably construe the words in a harsh and literal manner; while the more reasonable practice of the people would be treated by others from ignorance of the interpretations of the commentators as a custom contrary to the law.

Major Sparks, in s. 68 of his Code, ruled as follows:—"In the division of an "estate between the surviving husband or wife and children, the widow or widower "shall take the dwelling-house and three-fourths of the estate, and the children "divide the remaining one-fourth equally among them." This ruling is contested in 1873 by Mr. Sutherland, a Moulmein Advocate, in reply to Mr. Sandford's circular 15 of the 26th October 1872 about printing of Dhammathats. The Advocate defines "the true intention of the law, that a division of the estate is not to be made be- "fore the death of the widower or widow, except by consent, which, so far as I am "aware, is in practice carried out to the present day; and that the rights of children "in the estate generally as against their own father or mother virtually amount to "and are treated as merely possible rights contingent on the parents' death."

The case on inheritance appended to III Notes on Buddhist law shows that the disposition of property on the death of one parent is not yet settled by decisions; and that the most violent differences of opinion exist among Burmese judges as to the nature of the widow's estate. The distinction between ancestral and joint and separate acquisitions has not been taken, and Major Sparks gives no countenance to the paternal power conceded by the Dhammathats of wholly or partially disinheriting a son of bad character or destitute of merit. But in the recent correspondence about wills, many Burmans urge that a *paterfamilias* should be allowed by writing to pass such judgments on his children and affect the distribution accordingly. They claim this power as a right under the Dhammathats and treat the document as a mere convenience. In the same correspondence many appeal to the Dhammathat as authority for what they consider a rule far more reasonable than the uniform rule of Major Sparks : the rule which makes differences in the shares according to the ages of the children. In these two matters we find the ideas of the people closely approaching those of the ancient Hindu legislators, but until we give our officials some index to the source of these ideas and point out their antiquity, it is probable that they would be ignored. Yet there is nothing inequitable in apportionment among wards according to their necessities, and it is an open question whether the father or the Extra Assistant Commissioner may be best trusted with such duties. The Hindu law is stated by Colebrooke as follows, 5 Dig. 86 :—If the father be living, greater or less shares are received through his choice in proportion to duty, or piety, or the like : but after his death equal shares alone are received without attending to duty, or piety, or the like.

The rule given by Apastamba and intended to exhort householders to make a division during their lifetime, as later they ought to become hermits or ascetics, is thus translated by Dr. Bühler :—He should, during his lifetime, divide his wealth equally among his sons, excepting the eunuch, the madman, and the outcast.

For a judicial decision about an adopted daughter's rights to partition, *see* Ma Goon's case in Sandford's Rulings, page 30. Partition during the parents' lifetime is a topic closely bordering on gift. The limitations at Hindu law are thus stated by Mr. Justice West in "Narbadabai *vs.* Mahadeo" (I. L. R. 5 Bombay, 106) : "A "gift to a son by a Hindu parent must ordinarily be sustained. But, as amongst " the sons having a birthright in the estate, it is not to be grossly unfair. Even as " to self-acquired property, it is prescribed that the acquirer shall not part with it " so as to leave his family destitute."

S. 11. Bracelets, rings, earrings, necklaces, given to the daughter by her parents during the lifetime of the father shall be given to the daughter alone. The family of slaves, cows, and buffaloes by pairs shall also be divided. Indian-corn, peas, and paddy shall be given to the daughter as much as she deserves, and the balance to the mother. If the daughter be married and lives in a separate house, she alone is entitled to all things given her by her parents at the time of her marriage. If the daughter be one who eats and lives together with her parents, though she be from a respectable family, the mother being with her has the control over all the property. The mother of such daughter can make use of the property, can feed a second husband, and can make offerings, and even if the whole property become exhausted she cannot be blamed. If asked why the girl who is from a respectable family should not get any property by her being together with her parent, the reply is that the mother has control over her daughter. If the mother during her lifetime makes use of all the property and the property becomes exhausted, let it be so, but if any property be left the daughter alone takes possession of the said property. Therefore she who lives with her parent has to remain without anything before.

Note.—The property mentioned in this section as given to the daughter suggests that it is a kind of stridhan, on which subject the texts of Gautama, Apastamba, Vishnu, and Katyayana may be compared.

Devala.—Food and vesture, ornaments, perquisites, and wealth received by a woman from a kinsman are her own property; she may enjoy it herself.

Vasishtha.—The paraphernalia of the mother her female issue shall inherit in equal shares.

S. ˙12.   The following is the mode of dividing inheritance property between the father and the daughter after the death of the mother. The daughter alone is entitled to the ornaments and slaves given by both mother and father, in other words (*kyamin*) toilet ornaments. She (the daughter) is also entitled to all the valuable clothing and ornaments used by the mother, to cows and buffaloes by pairs, to ten milk-giving cows, 20 she-goats, and the female slave cook. The father alone is entitled to all the remaining property. Although it has thus been said, the father should give to the daughter things which she deserves.

Note.—In Bk. 6, s. 30, of the *Menu Kyay* the desertion of parents is punished as a crime : " If children do not minister to their parents, but leave them and live " separately, let all their property be taken from them, and they may be punished "criminally to the extent of 600 stripes of a rattan." The wife and the diseased children or brethren are also as in Hindu law declared to be entitled to maintenance. The notion of desert, learning, and virtue constituting claims to pre-eminence and the opposite qualities creating a bar to inheritance are too well known to the Hindu law to make reference necessary. The following reasons are found by the Buddhist compiler of laws for the doctrine that children inherit according to deserts :—

Menu Kyay, Bk. 10, s. 71.—" The law when property which ought to be treated as inheritance, but which has not been divided as such, shall be given to the person who deserves it, is this : If the parents who are rich give all their property to their children or grandchildren, and these children do not support them after having obtained the property, let the property be taken back as it was given, and let the person, whether relative or stranger, who supports the parents have the whole. The following is the precedent on which a stranger receives the property in this way :— Danentsia, the wealthy, had much property, the whole of which he gave to his children and trusted to them for support; after a time his daughter-in-law, the wife of his son, from her parsimonious disposition, failed to support him and he fell into a state of destitution. When the king was journeying through his dominions, he cunningly took a staff and begging-pot, and pretending to beg posted himself at a place where the king could see him ; the king enquired of his servants who it was that was begging with the staff and begging-pot ; they reported to the royal ear that it was Danentsia, the wealthy ; when the king heard this he returned to the palace, and on his arrival sent for the wealthy man and questioned him, who stated truly what had occurred. The king then sent for his sons and daughters, and on questioning them they also told him the same story ; on hearing which he said, ' the children are neglectful of their parents, and having taken much property do not support them.' Saying thus, he took all the property from the sons and daughters-in-law and supported the wealthy man himself, and at his death the sons and daughters-in-law did not inherit his property. People who have property, taken under a pledge to support the donor, and who do not do so, shall not inherit the property they may (by consanguinity) be entitled to ; as the king supported (the rich man) and inherited (his property), so the person who actually supports another shall inherit the property without reference to who he may be."

See also s. 87.   With ss. 11 and 12 of the *Wonnana* the *Menu Kyay*, Bk. 10, may be compared.   Here we find that the right of primogeniture, which is denied to women in the institutes of Manu, is allowed to the eldest daughter.

S. 4.   Oh excellent king, when a father dies there are two laws for the partition of the property between the mother and daughter, which are these :   Let the daughter have one female slave, two milch-cows, two milch-goats, one young male and female buffalo, one pay of grain land, and all the seed, vetches, paddy, corn, barley, sat, mayau, and sessamum.   Let the mother and younger daughters take all the residue of the property, animate and inanimate. The price of a female slave is seven tickals of siver and a half; a cow and a calf, three tickals each; the goat and kid, one and a half·tickals each; the male buffalo, five tickals; the female, two and a half; the pay of land, twenty tickals; and all the seed grain, two and a half tickals of silver. If one of the things now mentioned, and of which the price has been fixed, are in possession, if only gold and silver and other property is left, let the price now laid down be paid to the eldest daughter instead. If there be not the full number of cows and goats and there be ten buffaloes, the last only shall be divided; let the others that do not amount to this number be left out of the partition. A division shall only be made when there are three or four female slaves, the buffaloes, cows, and goats, and twenty-five pays of land; this is when the mother shall not take a second husband. If the mother has consumed the whole for necessary subsistence, let her have the right to do so. If the partition be made after the mother has taken another husband, let all the father's clothes and ornaments be divided into four portions, three of which the mother and younger daughters shall take, and let the fourth be given to the eldest daughter; let the mother have the house. The property, animate and inanimate, given to the eldest daughter shall be noted before witnesses, and (they) shall take care of it; and if the mother dies, let the eldest daughter have the property above allotted to her. Let the property brought by the mother be divided into four lots; let the step-father have one, and the eldest daughter and relations (brothers and sisters) three. The property brought by the step-father and his debts shall not be divided. The house shall be valued and the price divided into four parts, of which let the step·father have one, and let the house go to the eldest daughter, because it is the property of her parents.

S. 5.   Oh excellent king, when the father has died, the two laws for the partition of the inheritance between the mother and the sons are these: Let the eldest son have the riding horse, elephant, goblet, betel apparatus, sword, clothes, and ornaments, and of the slaves, the betel-carrier and two water-carriers; and let the mother have her clothes and ornaments, goblet, betel apparatus, and all the female slaves. Let the residue be divided into four parts, of which let the eldest son have one and the mother and younger children three. This is the law when the mother does not marry again. If the mother uses the property for necessary subsistence, let her have the right to do so. If the mother takes another husband, the portion of the eldest son, animate and inanimate, shall be noted before witnesses and taken care of; and if he be too young to separate from his parents and the mother dies, let him have all that has been apportioned to him above, and having divided the portion of the mother into four parts, let the step-father have one part and eldest son three. The original property and the debts of the step-father shall not be divided, but of the mother's original debts let the step-father pay one-fourth; having valued the house, let the step-father have one-fourth. Why is this? Because it was the house of the son's parents.

S. 11.   In case of the father's death and the sons demanding their inheritance from the mother, the two laws for the partition of one-fourth share amongst the relations: Let the eldest son have the father's elephant, horse, clothes, ornaments, betel apparatus, sword and goblet, and let the residue of the property at the mother's death be divided amongst the relations (to brothers and sisters of the eldest son?); it must not be divided till her death.

S. 12.   In case of the mother's death and the daughters demanding their inheritance of their father, the same rule holds as above laid down.

S. 13(*a*).   The following shall be considered the rule of inheritance between the father and the sons on the death of the mother. The son knows not about the property. The mother and father only made the property increase for their own maintenance and the maintenance of their sons and grandchildren. The mother alone takes charge of the property brought by the father from a distant place. The son is entitled to the things given him during the lifetime of both husband and wife. If such property be still in possession, the mother and father who have become poor have the right to take the property back. Mother and father who have a great number of sons and daughters complete (all living) and have a lot of property and then again become poor, *the children* shall sell their own bodies and support their mother and father. When the parents are in adversity those sons should also share in it, and when in prosperity those sons shall enjoy the inheritance of the mother and father.

(*b*). The sons are entitled to get what is given them in infancy by their mother and father. They shall also each choose and take one of the articles left in the house of the mother. They shall also get buffaloes and cows by pairs, one milk-giving cow and a bull, twenty she-goats, and a fighting he-goat. The father alone is entitled to all the remaining property. Though this has been said the father shall give to the sons what they deserve.

Note.—Gift is as at Hindu law the fourth of the 18 titles and is found in the Compendium, Bk. 2, of the *Menu Kyay* : again in Bk. 8, ss. 3 and 4, in great detail : and again mixed up with the duties of children at the end of Bk. 10. *See* also ss. 22, 23, and 24 of Bk. 10. The giving of children in adoption and marriage and the giving of a wife are sometimes treated under " Gift." The following, which has somehow got into s. 30 of Bk. 6, is quoted as interesting and argumentative :—
" If the parents of a young man and woman, at the time of betrothing them, shall place their hands together in a cup of water and say that they give to this daughter and son-in-law, or this son and daughter-in-law, gold, silver, gems, iron, property animate or inanimate, elephants, horses, buffaloes, oxen, slaves or lands, and there be witnesses to the gift, nevertheless the children have no right to demand of the parents anything not given in hand, they have only a right to the property actually made over to them ; if they expend the whole of that, let them have a right to do so ; if they do not expend the whole and the parents take back what remains, they have a right to do so ; the children shall not claim it on the ground of its being a gift and being in possession. If the son or daughter should die, let the survivor have all the property brought at the time of marriage, but shall have no claim to anything that was promised, or anything that did not actually come into their possession. If the children have gone to a separate establishment, their relations (co-heirs, brothers, and sisters) shall have no claim to any property they have taken with them. If not given them by their parents at the death of the latter, let this property be their own separate share. If the parents be not dead and their daughter (the wife) shall die, her parents shall not say they did not give her this property, but only wished that their daughter and son-in-law might enjoy the use of it during their lives ; they shall have no right to take it back on these grounds. Why is this ? Because the daughter is dead. If the parents of the husband on his death shall say they did not give him the property, but that he had taken their property with him to his own separate residence and was using it, they shall not on this ground obtain the property that is in the possession of their daughter-in-law. Why is this ? Because, when the wife dies, the husband takes the property. In another case : If, on the ground of being the eldest, a son or daughter has taken much of their parents' property without its having been given to them, let it on the death of the parents be divided with the relations ; it shall not be their separate share. Why is this ? Because the eldest brother is in the place of the property left, and when the husband dies the wife takes it. In father, and the eldest sister of the mother, to their younger brothers and sisters. If any man shall give his wife to another in the presence of witnesses, the man to whom she is given has a right to her. If, before he has had connection with her, her former husband shall demand her back, and she be willing to return to him, let him pay the price of her body to the man to whom she has been given, and on paying this he may take her back. If the wife say, he has given me away to another man, I will not return to him, let her be free ; he shall have no claim to her. Why is this ? Because his engagement would be broken."
In the case of " Mra Do Oung *vs.* Shway Oo " (Rulings 19) Sandford J., after stating the Burmese law about gift, refused to be bound by it where it was inconsistent with justice and required evidence of implied trust or condition that the donee

2

was to support the donor. For cases of gifts to children on entering the priesthood, see pages 27 and 42 of the Rulings. The learned Judge inferred that the Buddhist law, like the Hindu, requires transfer of possession to make a gift complete, except in the special case of a gift made to a child on his entering the priesthood. For the relation of the Contract Act to the religious law of joint-family see " Samulbhai *vs.* Somsshwar," I.L.R. 4 Bombay, 38. I do not here discuss the nature of the estate taken by the widow or widower or the rights of children and others to maintenance. The exact meaning of the written law, especially the words used for different sorts of property, has yet to be determined on comparison of the Pali texts, and it is possible that these latter may be based on Sanscrit originals.

S. 14. If the mother and father sell or pledge a son to another person and if the mother and father die, and if there is a great quantity of property, gold and silver, left, let the value of the body (of the son sold) be deducted from the inheritance property, and let the son thus sold receive two parts of the remainder, the reason is because *the parents* died in prosperity. If the parents died in adversity, the son sold shall not tell the elder brothers that they are wicked or good, upright or mean, that they ought to pay for or redeem his body, and that he should get a share in the property.

Note.—Under the Burmese law parents might sell their children when in want as we see from the *Menu Kyay*, Bk. 3, s. 59, Bk. 7, ss. 35 and 39, also s. 26, where the whole subject of slavery is elaborately discussed. The eldest son often stepped into the rights and duties of his father, as we see in s. 22 of Bk. 10 and in s. 41 below. Since the abrogation of slavery and the enactment of the Penal Code, the British Courts would refuse to recognize that institution, but I have been told that in the Mergui district parents occasionally hire out their daughters for a term of years.

S. 15. If the eldest brother sells or pledges his youngest brother, and if the eldest brother has no sons, grandchildren, or heirs, the youngest brother sold is entitled to take and enjoy all the inheritance property of the brother. If after the eldest brother has sold *the youngest brother*, the mother and father again sell *him* to another person, he shall not say " I alone am concerned, and I alone am entitled to my eldest brother's property," in other words, if the eldest brother sell his young brother, even if he has sons, after his death the young brother, who by his being sold and mortgaged supported *the eldest brother*, only is entitled to all the inheritance property.

S. 16. Oh highest of the race of the sun, royal and ruling lord, if sons and daughters are well-to-do and their mother and father poor, *they* should support that mother and father. If they do not support, the rulers and judges should ask *the children* the value of their bodies and give it *to the mother and father*. Although this has been said, *even if the children* are sold during their childhood, they should not say that they have not been supported. Though it has been said *that the parents* are undeserving, yet it is only through their respect *that the children got on*, and therefore if they (children) be in prosperity *they* should with reverence support their mother and father.

S. 17. The following is the way of dividing the ancestral property among the children born of the same parents after their (mi-pa) parents' death. The eldest son shall receive two shares, the elder one-and-a-half shares, the youngest one share. The shares of the eldest, elder, and youngest daughters shall be in the same proportion as those of the eldest, elder, and youngest sons. The eldest son and the eldest daughter shall receive their share of cattle in the same proportion. This law of division applies to unmarried children.

Note.—This rule is repeated in s. 41: see also s. 64. The rule in the *Menu Kyay* is as follows :—

Bk. 10, s. 14.—In case of the death of both father and mother and their leaving only sons : After the eldest son has taken the clothes and ornaments of the father, let all the residue of the property, animate and inanimate, with the mother's clothes and ornaments, be divided into ten parts, and let the eldest son have one ; let the residue be again divided into ten, and let the second have one share ; let the remainder be again divided into ten, and let the other children each have a share ; and let the rest be divided equally amongst all. In this case also it has been laid down that the division into ten shall be repeated seven times, and here also some must be set apart for religious offerings.

If the father and mother both die, leaving male and female children, let the eldest son have the clothes and ornaments of the father and the eldest daughter the clothes and ornaments of the mother; the residue of the property, animate and inanimate, shall be divided into fifteen shares, and let each take one according to age; having added them together and divided them three times, let the residue then be divided equally. In this case also seven divisions have been ordered prior to the equal distribution of the residue. Here also a portion must be set aside for religious offerings.

I give the rules about survivorship and partition between undivided unmarried brethren as stated in the *Menu Kyay*. The division of profits according to amount of capital is based on the same principle as s. 170 of the *Wonnana*, which seems to have been left out of Bk. 12 of the *Menu Kyay* about divorce.

Bk. 10, s. 57.—The law of inheritance between a younger and elder brother : If a younger and elder brother living together shall acquire property, and the elder shall die, let the younger take the whole, and if the younger die, let the elder have the whole, and let them pay the debts in the same proportion ; this is when neither has a wife or family.

If the same living together shall equally contribute to the acquisition of property, let them divide it equally. If the original capital shall have been the property of one only, and there shall have been a profit, let the principal be paid to him to whom it belongs and the profits divided equally. If the two live together, and the youngest assist the elder, and be the most influential person of the two, let him have two-thirds profit and the elder one. If the elder be the principal person, in the same way let him have two, and (the younger) one share. If, whilst so living together, one shall have bad health and the other shall take care of him, let him have only his food and clothes.

The result is similar under s. 17 of the *Wonnana* to what occurs under the rule of Manu's Institutes interpreted by Colebrooke, V. Dig. 39, and *see* 35 as to intermediate children. The daughter's estate appears to be equal to the son's, and there is no suggestion of the *appointed* daughter of the old Hindu law or of postponement to male relations.

According to Vishnu, mothers of different classes shall receive shares proportionate to their sons' shares, and so shall unmarried daughters, Colebrooke V, 86. In s. 17 of the *Wonnana* we find the Hindu rule about sons extended to daughters, and apparently the other Hindu rule which gives priority to the unmarried daughter is adopted. The question is where and when did the law originate which conferred such great rights on females ? There is no suggestion as in the Hindu books of the brothers paying the unmarried girls' marriage expenses out of the property. But according to some commentators the allotment of a share answered the same purpose. For an account of the history of women's rights of inheritance at Hindu law, *see* " Bhau Nanaji *vs.* Sundrabai " (11 Bombay, 249), where the subject and that of proof of custom is discussed by West J.

S. 18. Besides this, the following should be the mode of division between sons. The eldest shall first choose and take one of the articles from amongst the gold and silver; after this the property shall be divided into ten parts and the eldest son, who had taken what he liked, shall take one part. The balance shall be again divided into ten parts and the next mother's own and pretty son shall take one part. In this manner the property shall be divided into ten parts over and over again as the number of sons may be, allowing each son to take one part in his turn till each son has received his share. The balance after thus dividing shall be equally divided between them all.

Note.—See the quotation from the *Menu Kyay* in note to s. 17. The rule about taking the best chattel is found in Gautama, but I have not found in the Indian books any rule providing for the repeated divisions.

S. 19. If only daughters are born, the eldest daughter shall first choose and take one of the articles from amongst the gold and silver. After the eldest sister has thus taken, let the property be divided into twenty parts and let the eldest sister, who had taken what she liked, take one part. Let the balance be again divided into twenty parts and let the next mother's own and pretty daughter take one part. In this manner the property should be divided over and over again till all the daughters have received their shares. Let the balance be equally divided amongst them.

Note.—The *Menu Kyay* gives the following rule :—
" *Bk. 10, s. 13.* In case of the death of both father and mother, and there be only female children, let the eldest daughter have all the mother's clothes and orna-ments, and let the father's clothes and all other property, animate and inanimate, be divided into twenty shares, of which let the eldest daughter take one ; then let the residue be again divided into twenty, and let the second daughter have one share ; let the residue be for the third time divided into twenty, and each of the other children have one share ; and let the residue after this be equally divided amongst all. It has also been said by my lord hermit that the division (into twenty) should be repeated seven times and then the equal division made ; but a portion of the property must be first set aside for religious purposes on the parents' account."
But the case of six daughters in s. 72 of Bk. 10 is specially treated : see also s. 34, *ibid.*, and s. 34 below.

S. 20. If during the lifetime of both mother and father the eld-est son dies and leaves sons, the eldest shall get as much as the youngest son (*i.e.*, his youngest uncle). If the eldest grandchild dies and the next grandchild is living, let his father's share he divided into four parts and let him receive one part.

Note.—In a Hindu undivided family, the interest of the deceased co-parcener would vest in his son or grandson. The writer of the *Menu Kyay* gives the reason for the rules in this and the next sections :—
" *Bk. 10, s. 15.*—If the eldest son dies before his father and mother, the law of inheritance between his son and his son's uncles and aunts is this : Because in case of the death of father and mother the eldest son (awratha) is called father, let his son and his (the eldest son's) younger brothers share alike.
" Should the eldest daughter die before the father and mother, this is the law for the partition of the inheritance between her daughter and her daughter's uncles and aunts : That the daughter of the eldest daughter and her (the eldest daughter's) younger sisters shall share alike, because the eldest daughter, when grown up, stands in the place of a mother.
" In case of the death of the younger children occurring before the parents, the law for partition of the inheritance between their children and the (co-heirs) relations of their parents is this : The children of the deceased have one-fourth of the share which would have come to their parents."

S. 21. In the same manner if the eldest daughter dies and leaves sons, the *eldest* shall get as much as the youngest sister (*i.e.*, youngest aunt). If the eldest grandchild dies and the next grandchild is living, let his mother's share be divided into four parts and let that second grandchild from that deceased daughter receive one part, the reason is because his *mother* was not *living* to have received *her share* of inheritance.

S. 22. The following are those not entitled to inherit whether or not living :—Grandfather and grandmother, likewise great-grand-children, great-great-grandchildren, great-great-great-grandchildren, step-mothers, step-fathers, uncles (father's younger brothers), big uncles (father's elder brothers), big aunts (mother's elder sisters), grandmothers, grandfathers, and great-grandfathers.

Note.— For fuller explanation consult ss. 45 and 46 below and the *Menu Kyay*, Bk. 10, ss. 18 and 19. For a curious case of a separated husband and wife dividing the property of their deceased children living separately from them, I refer the reader to s. 81 of the same book. The precedent for that case is that of the wild pigeons : when the jungle was on fire the male bird carried off the male young one and the female the female. The precedent of the woman who bore a snake, who demanded his share of inheritance, has also endeared itself to the people if we may judge to the references made to it in their replies about wills. Such of the hpiatthoons, or legendary decisions, as have been embodied in the Dhammathats ought to be taken for what they are worth : their value is far higher than those which the compilers refrained from inserting and which are not known to have received the force of law.

According to s. 33 of the *Menu Kyay*, Bk. 10, as interpreted by the Special Court in " Mee Pyne *vs.* Mee Htoo " (page 86 of Christopher) a great-grandson is entitled to share in the undivided estate of his great-grandfather.

S. 23. If after the death of the mother the father marries a lesser wife and then the father also dies, the following should be the mode of division between the son by the first marriage and his step-mother. The son is entitled to three portions of the property brought by *his* mother and father, and as the step-mother has been the wife of the father she is entitled to one portion. The son by the second marriage shall get two portions of the (လက်ထက်ပွား) letthetpwa property (property acquired by both after marriage), the son by the first marriage one portion, and the step-mother five portions. The property brought by the father shall be divided into five portions and the son shall receive four portions and the step-mother one portion. Thus it has also been decided.

Note.—Compare *Menu Kyay*, Bk. 10, s. 7, and for the cases of three successive wives and husbands ss. 66 and 67.

S. 24. After the death of the mother the father marries a lesser wife and then both the husband and wife die, the mode of division of property between the son of the two marriages is as follows :—
The son brought by the father (son by the first marriage) shall alone receive all the property brought by the father. The son by the lesser wife shall alone receive all the (ပါရင်း payin) property origi-nally brought by his mother. After leaving out sufficient amount for offerings, the lesser wife's son shall receive two portions and the son by the first marriage one portion of the (လက်ထက်ပွား letthetpwa) property acquired by both.
The division between the sons by the first marriage shall be pro-portionally made. The sons by the second marriage shall receive two

portions as the mother is their own. The sons by the first marriage shall only receive one portion as the father alone *is their own.* The sons by the former husband are entitled to his (former husband's) property and the sons by the second husband are entitled to his (second husband's) property.

If there are clothing and ornaments given to the wife by the father of the *man* (*i.e.*, father-in-law), the sons shall not snatch away anything given by the father. Thus it has also been decided.

Note.—The bride's fee is known to the eldest Hindu period, being mentioned by Gautama, and included (sulka) among stridhan by Vishnu. According to Dr. Bühler it was originally |the price due to the parents or guardian of the bride for surrendering her to the bridegroom and became in after-times a wedding present, which the bride received from the bridegroom, either directly or through her parents.

S. 25. When the property acquired before marriage is of small amount and the property acquired after marriage is of large amount, the property acquired by the husband and the wife by luck and industry should be divided into five (equal) portions. The son (child) of the wife by her former husband is entitled to one portion ; the son (child) of the husband by his former wife is entitled to one portion ; and the son (child) of both husband and wife is entitled to three portions. If no property be acquired after marriage, the property of the wife and of the husband being divided into five *equal* portions, the sons (children) of both the husband and the wife should each receive one portion ; and the step-sons (children) should each receive four portions. In this manner ought the inheritance of the daughters and sons living and eating together be apportioned.

Note.—The first case is similarly dealt with by s. 9 of Bk. 10 of the *Menu Kyay* : the treatment of the second case differs. For the interpretations of Sandford J. over-ruling Major Sparks' Code, see page 14 of Rulings.

S. 26. If at the death of the father, the mother, having equally divided the inheritance with the sons (children) and taking her half share, marries a second husband and unites her property with that of the second husband, the second husband alone owns her property at her death, for, each having received his or her share, it is the mother's property and the children have no claim thereto.

S. 27. If the husband dies without issue, the young wife should own the whole property. Similarly if the wife dies without issue and the husband is left, he should own the whole property. An inheritance consisting only of gold or silver, auimate or inanimate things, and slaves ought thus to be apportioned among wives and children.

Note.—In Cunningham's Digest of Hindu law the rule is thus stated :—" The " widow of a man who dies without male issue and has no coparcener is entitled " to succeed to his property ancestral and self-acquired." But in Bengal the widow inherits whether her husband was separated from the joint family or not.

S. 28. Rule regarding hereditary succession. Let the eldest son succeed the father at his death. When the eldest brother dies the younger brother should succeed. This ought to be the order of succession. Similarly in hereditary succession with women, when the mother dies her daughter ought to succeed her. If the eldest daughter be dead, the younger daughters should succeed according to their age.

Note.—This perhaps refers to honours and impartible estate, or to the right of managing joint concerns, or possibly it contains a trace of a separate rule for woman's property. An exception is made in the *Menu Kyay*, Bk. 10, ss. 35 and 36, of hermaphrodites and diseased sons, similar to the Hindu law of exclusion from inheritance, the ideas belonging to which recur in regard to abuse, void marriages, supersession after marriage, &c. *See* s. 44 below and my Note III on the *Wonnana*.

S. 29. When the son and the father are dead, the surviving wife alone is entitled to the whole estate, and it is her duty to liquidate debts. She must also lay aside (a portion) for offerings, and if there be sons (children) unmarried, she must reserve a sufficient portion for the ceremony of washing the head, and such like purposes. Whatever remains the wife alone may apply to her own use.

Note.—At Hindu law the widow who took the estate was to offer sacrifices and provide for the marriage of unmarried daughters.

S. 30. If, on apportioning the estate, any of the heirs be absent his share should be reserved for him. If any *of the heirs* die before the estate is apportioned, his sons (children) and wife should receive his portion. If he have no wife or child, his share should be divided proportionally amongst those relatives of the mother and father who live together.

Note.—See s. 56 below. The rules of limitation are more fully stated at the end of the rules about inheritance in Bk. 10 of the *Wonnana*. The Special Court has decided in two cases reported in Christopher that the Burmese law cannot be enforced when it conflicts with the Limitation Acts.

S. 31. In the absence of heirs, the whole estate should be equally divided between the hettima son and the person dependent (upon the deceased). If that man does not receive his share of the estate, judges should pass a judgment ordering *the share* to be given to that man.

Note.—See section 5.

S. 32. If the son of the elder wife be young and the son of the lesser wife old, a bull should be given to the elder and (the estate) be divided according to relationship.

Note.—Compare with ss. 36 to 38 of the *Menu Kyay*, Bk. 10. That Dhammathat does nowhere allude to the giving of the bull : the following quotation shows the Hindu origin. [*Gautama.*—If a man has several wives, the additional share of the eldest son is one bull (in case he be born of a later-married wife.)] *See* also 14 Moore's Indian Appeals, 570, and 5 Bombay H. C. R. 161, A. C. J.

S. 33. If there be sons and daughters (children) by six different classes of wives, the children by the wife of the kingly class are entitled to four portions ; the children by the wife of the Brahmin class three portions ; the children by the wife of the merchant class two portions ; the children by the wife of the agricultural class one portion ; and similarly the children of the soldier or military class one portion. One class of teachers (lawgivers) say that children by a wife of the mean class should receive half a portion. If there be no children by the five classes of wives mentioned above, the son by the wife of the mean class should receive at the death of the mother and father two portions and other sons (children) one portion.

Note.—See ss. 3 and 4 above.

S. 34. If mother and father, after having seven daughters born to them, get a son, *the property* shall be equally divided between the brother and sisters, in other words, they shall get as much as they deserve. If these brothers and sisters are born alternately, the eldest sister shall get as much as the eldest brother, the elder sister as much as the elder brother, and the young sister as much as the young brother, in the proportion of two, one-and-a-half, one, and half a share respectively. On the other hand, if the son is the firstborn and then the daughter is born, the son shall take all the articles used by the father and the daughter all those used by the mother. After the son and daughter have each taken thus, let the son receive only two parts of the residue; and as for the sister the correct amount is one-and-a-half parts *as in the former case.*

Note.—See s. 19 above and compare with ss. 34 and 72 of the *Menu Kyay,* Bk. 10.

S. 35. If a person uses inheritance property for trading purposes, though it be for months or years, yet no interest shall be charged, as it was not a debt. If sons and relatives, who are heirs to the estate, cause the increase of the inheritance by trading, all the profits should be reasonably valued and divided proportionally.

Note.—This is more fully stated in s. 68 : see also the *Menu Kyay,* ss. 79 and 80 ; and for the Hindu law 10 Moore's Indian appeals, 490.

S. 36. If a person obtains property by his own wisdom, or by asking from friends, he shall get such property. He who obtained the property shall take the whole, and others shall not have any share in it. If the mother and father during their lifetime give certain property to the sons and daughters, all that property ought not to be shared. Though it has been thus said, if a large amount of property be given to those sons and daughters, the giving not being equal, all that was given should be calculated, and being divided and distributed should be put into each *person's* share. On the other hand, if the mother and father give certain property to certain sons and daughters and if there be no residue, such property should be divided as inheritance ; the reason is because if a mother hen brings food and gives it to one of the chickens, the other chickens will also snatch and eat it ; therefore the division should be the same, for the single chicken was not allowed to eat the food brought by the mother hen.

Note.—This rule is repeated in s. 43: see also s. 48. A similar subject is discussed in Note I of this series, para. 45. As to division of acquired property between brothers, see s. 57 of the *Menu Kyay,* Bk. 10: and ss. 79 and 80 for acquisitions on other trading capitals. The simile of the hen and chickens occurs in s. 78 and at the end of s. 81 of the *Menu Kyay* : and perhaps the verb *snatch* refers to the same thing in other passages. The passage here at once suggests the

Hiudu law, *e. g.*, *Vyasa*. Wealth acquired by learning, or gained by valour, or received from affectionate kindred, belongs, when partition is made, to him who acquired it, and shall not be claimed by the co-heirs.

S. 37. Property given away at marriage shall be owned by that son and daughter. The other daughters and sons shall not snatch away (claim) that property. Property given otherwise shall be divided. If those persons have sons and daughters, (they) the grand-children shall get as much as they deserve out of the property given to the married son and daughter (their mother and father). The division shall be proportionally made.

Note.—See the comment on s. 13.

S. 38. If a person abducts and takes away to a distant place the daughter of another person and gets a son by her, and they with the property jointly acquired by them (လက်ထက်ပွား။ letthetpwa) buy a slave, and if unluckily thereafter the husband should die, the slave shall then go to the mother and father of his mistress to ask them for the hand of their daughter (the widow of the slave's deceased master). On the mother and father consenting, the slave takes the mistress to be his wife, and begets sons and daughters by her. The slave husband also unfortunately dies, the sons born afterwards (during this marriage) only are entitled to the estate of the mother and father. The son born during the union to which the *parents* were not consenting parties is not entitled to inherit. If even the grandfather and grandmother and others did not consent (to the union), was it not by consent of his own mother and father, and nevertheless why should not that first son share? It is because he is not included among those sons who are entitled to inherit. Although it has been said that he shall not share, this has reference only to the estate of the grandmother and grandfather. This is our opinion. Learned men have said that such sons shall get an equal share of the property acquired during the slave-father's lifetime, after the death of the step-father, and the mother and father, so nothing need be said as regards his own father's property.

Note.—See s. 122 of the *Wonnana* in Note III: also s. 73 of the *Menu Kyay*, Bk. 10, for this case, and ss. 51 to 53 of the same.

S. 39. A woman who has lost her husband makes a slave her husband and gets sons and daughters by him, and the property and slaves increase. On the death of both all the property acquired afterwards (ရှာတက်ပွား။) shall be equally divided between the sons by the first husband and the sons by the slave-husband.

Note.—See ss. 44 and 45 of the *Menu Kyay*, Bk. 10, for fuller treatment of such cases.

S. 40. If there is only one son and several wives, the son alone shall get more. If there is no son and if *the wives* be not of different classes but of the same, *the property* shall be equally divided between them.

Note.—See ss. 4 and 33 above.

3

S. 41. In other words, if there are only unmarried brothers and sisters, the young sons (children) shall pay the same respect to their eldest brother and sister as to their mother and father and shall in return support them. At the division of the mother and father's estate, the cows and goats shall first be given to the eldest person in excess. The eldest brother shall receive two parts of the residue, the eldest sister one-and-a-half parts, and the young sons and daughters each one part. Although the inheritance has been divided, the eldest son shall support the youngest brother. The youngest brother shall also *in his turn* respect and treat the eldest brother as if he were the father. If the eldest brother, being avaricious, takes the young brother's share, that eldest brother shall receive criminal punishment and he shall not receive the articles used by his father.

S. 42. If young sons say "give us our share in the estate, we "will live in separate houses or will give the value of charitable offer- "ings;" if such a son carry the responsibility of the mother and father, and if he be the eldest son, *let the estate* be divided into two shares, and let him first take the share he prefers and let the residue be divided into nine shares, and let the said eldest brother again take one share. Let the residue be again divided into nine shares, and let the younger brother receive one share. Let the residue be again divided into nine shares, and let the eldest brother receive one share, and let the younger brother receive all the remaining. This is the mode of division between two brothers.

If there be an elder sister *also*, let the younger brother's share be divided into four parts, and let that eldest sister first receive one part. The eldest son shall first get the Burmese and Kala (foreign) goats. The elephants, horses, oxen and buffaloes, peacocks and male deer shall be equally divided between him or her *as the case may be* and the younger brother. As regards *division of* things given during the lifetime *of the parents*, the mode has already been shown. Let the eldest son receive two parts, the elder son one-and-a-half parts, and the young son one part. Thus in this manner also learned men have decided.

S. 43. If mother and father give property as capital to sons and daughters, the remaining sons (children) shall not snatch away such property. The sons and daughters of the sons and daughters who had received such property are only entitled to it.

Note.—This repeats s. 36.

S. 44. If amongst the sons of a couple regularly given in marriage by their parents one be a hermaphrodite, he shall not receive an equal share, but shall receive according to his merits.

S. 45. Grandfather and grandmother, father's younger brother and father's elder brother, are not entitled to the estate of the descendants. The sons and grandchildren only are entitled to it. If there be no own sons and grandchildren, the kittima son alone shall receive it. If there be no kittima son, the apatitha son alone is entitled to it; if there be no apatitha son, the mother, father, and relations shall be entitled to it. Teachers and pupils have like rules.

S. 46. The mother and father of children who have lived away from them shall not inherit the estate of the children, even if they (mother and father) be living, for the waters of a river never flow to the source, but downwards. If the sons and wife *or husband* (as the case may be) of that son and daughter be not living, the mother and father, &c., have a right to the estate. The reason is because it is likened to the waters which flow into the ocean, which is their destination. This is true. Though the waters have arrived at their destination they more or less, somehow or other, flow back to the source. If no mother and father or relations are living, then only shall the property go to Government (ဝင်းဘဏ္ဍာ).

Note.—See the note to s.22 above.

S. 47. If sons live and eat in separate houses, the same mode as *abovementioned* is laid down. If the sons have not been married, they shall support their mother and father. The sons who support their mother and father are entitled to be called awratha sons and shall therefore receive two portions. The son who bears the responsibility of the mother and father is entitled to the name of awratha whether he be the eldest or the young son. That son alone shall receive two portions. The son who lives and eats in a separate house shall receive half a portion.

S. 48. If *parents* give property to sons living in separate houses and to those living with them, and if such property be not exhausted and still be in possession, the father and mother can take back all the property thus given, if they wish it. If *such property* be exhausted, there shall be no return.

Note.—See note to s. 13, in which the judicial decisions are mentioned.

S. 49. Property given by the mother and father to the sons and daughters is of two kinds,—one which can be retained and the other which cannot be retained. There are also three kinds,—one which given can be retained, the other though given cannot be retained, and one though not given can be owned.

Note.—For a full discussion of this part of the law of gifts, see the rules about children's thengthee, or separate property, at the end of Bk. 10 of the *Menu Kyay*, and the important judgments of Mr. Sandford which modify the text. The twelve kinds of children's thengthee, according to the *Menu Kyay*, are as follows :—

(1) what is given to a child on being first put into its cradle ;
(2) what is given at the first shaving of the head ;
(3) what is given when the ears are bored ;
(4) what is given on betrothment ;
(5) what is given in illness ;
(6) what is given on entering the priesthood ;
(7) all gifts of ornaments, anklets, earrings, necklaces of kinds, bracelets ;
(8) what has been taken away and enjoyed separately without having been given by the parents ;
(9) gifts from grandparents ;
(10) gifts from affectionate regard by other people.
(11) whatever may have been acquired by their own skill, learning or wisdom ;
(12) gifts from my lord the king.

S. 50. Property given by *mother and father* to sons and daughters at the time of marriage can be retained by such sons and daughters if taken away with them. This is the kind of property which can be retained.

S. 51. If certain property be given *verbally*, but not received, and no note *of the giving* be kept, and not allowed to use the same, such property is said to be of the kind which though given cannot be retained.

S. 52. If animate and inanimate property without being *expressly* given comes to the possession, and the period of possession is known, and the said property made use of, this is the kind of property which though not given may be owned; all the property said to be thus entitled should not be included in the inheritance.

S. 53. If certain property belonging to the mother and father be kept undivided in the possession of some one or other for a long period (months and years), even if the descendants go down to the third generation, the inheritance should be divided; if it goes beyond the third generation, it, should not be divided; the reason is because the mother and father's descent ends at the third generation.

Note.—This rule differs from the *Menu Kyay*, Bk. 10, s. 33, which appears to allow partition at the instance even of a great-great-grandson in certain circumstances. As to the great-grandson, see the judgment of the Special Court mentioned in the note to s. 22 above. The rule of ı indu law is stated in Cunningham's Digest thus : The father, son, grandson or great grandson can enforce partition against all the other co-parceners and whether the majority of the co-parceners assent or not.

S. 54. If a man divorces his wife and surrenders all animate and inanimate property to her, the sons and daughters by the first wife (her) are not entitled to the property acquired after the *divorce*, only the daughters and sons by the second wife are entitled to it.

Note.—If the separating wife were pregnant and married again, the child would, according to the *Menu Kyay*, Bk. 10, s. 54, be entitled to a quarter of the second husband's ancestral estate and half of his mother's ancestral estate as well as two-fifths of the letthetpwa. The meaning of that section requires explanation. See also section 81 of the same book and Bk. 12 as to division on separation of married people.

S. 55. If the inheritance be divided among the son, grandchild, great-grandchild, and great-great-grandchild, those at a distance are entitled to one share and those near two shares. If *all* be away as visitors, the shares shall be equal, the reason is because it is likened to four pairs, *i.e.*, eight bullocks dragging a large log.

S. 56. After the division of the different kinds of inheritance property already stated, the claim for the shares shall be made within seven days. If the claim be not made within seven days, it should be made within thirty days. If the claim be not made within thirty days, none can be made after that date. If that person had gone to a far place, the claim should be made within three months; after that date no claim can be made. If claim be then made, it should not be considered a claim.

Note.—*See* note to s. 30 above.

S. 57. If a person feeds one with rice who is at the point of death and another tries to cure him with medicine, on the recovery of the sick man the price of his body should be divided into two portions, and one portion should be given to the physician and one to the person who fed him with rice. Learned men should always give decisions based on this rule.

Note.—In ss. 19 and 20 of Bk. 2 of the *Menu Kyay* the fee to the doctor who saves a man's life is 30 tickals of silver, in other cases three tickals. In s. 62 of Bk. 10 the relative who assists a sick person and buries him is said to be entitled to the whole inheritance in possession and to half of that not already vested.

S. 58. Oh lord ! mother and father on account of their affection give to the son, daughter-in-law, daughter, or son-in-law all the property, that son or daughter, &c., should, till the end of his or her life, support the father and mother. If he or she do not support, the *parents* are entitled to take back the whole property. If *persons* not related to the father and mother yet support them as if they were their own mother and father, they are entitled to a share of the inheritance. The claim of own children is indisputable.

Note.—See notes to ss. 12 and 13 above.

S. 59. A mother and father give (make a gift) to their children before their marriage of bracelets, rings, necklaces, or (other) such articles to wear, and on their marriage again give *the ornaments* to those still unmarried, three times giving the ornaments to the children in the order of age should be awaited for. If the father and mother die, the children in whose possession the ornaments then are are entitled to them.

S. 60. If a father and mother and grandfather and grandmother give certain property to prevent danger or quarrel, they should not when angry snatch (take) it back.

S. 61. If a (father and mother) give certain property to a son and daughter, and being angry resume it and give it to another son or daughter, the children to whom the property was first given are entitled to the property on the death of the father and mother. •

S. 62. At the time of our Phara (Buddha) a rich man knew which of his sons and grandchildren was not, and which was, meritorious and proficient in religious duties. That person alone should get the whole property. He (the rich man) kept his property with such intentions. Ah Shin Maha Ananda (the great saint Ananda) said that on the death of the rich man the son really related, alone, ought to receive the whole property, but Shin Oopahlee Htee (saint Oopahlee Htee) said that the grandchild who possessed the qualities in accordance with the rich man's intentions and request ought to get the whole property. Thus have the two disciples said.

Note.—See my notes to s. 10 and 12 above. In the papers about wills, Kyoungtaga Oo Tha Kway of Moulmein quotes this case as a precedent for the following conclusion. From the era of Gaudama up to the present time the custom obtains among the Buddhist Talaings and Burmans of giving away property before their death. Therefore if owners make a bequest of their property, either by oral promise before witnesses or by written wills, such bequest should be strictly observed.

63. The law of inheritance is abstruse, and various and different are the ways by which people are accustomed to divide a family estate. According as the law of inheritance is difficult, I shall illuminate its intricacy in a series of illustrations that wise men may profit thereby. If such a division of property be not expounded here, others will find themselves embarrassed when called upon to decide such cases. I will explain what the law on inheritance really is so that it may be easily understood. Though it is one of the most important portions of law, yet different Dhammathats have enacted different laws on it. I shall often recur to such disagreements of the Dhammathats. May good people listen to me. In the case of the division of an estate amongst a family of eight children born in the following order, first a daughter, then a son, then three daughters, then two sons, and lastly a daughter. I shall first divide these children into four divisions :—

(1) the first-born daughter and the son who is born next after her are called the " jetthas " (eldest) ;

(2) the daughters who are born as the third, fourth, and fifth children, and the sons who are born after the fifth child are called " majjhimas " (middle) ;

(3) the daughters who are born after four children and the sons who are born after six are called "kanitthas " (younger) ;

(4) the daughters who are born after five children and the sons who are born after eight are called " kuddakas " (youngest).

First of all the " jettha " sons shall get all the property used by the father (his personal property), and the " jettha " daughter shall get all the personal property and one female slave belonging to the mother. The property that remains shall be divided into twenty shares and the " jettha " daughters shall obtain two shares. Similarly the remaining property shall again be divided into twenty shares and the " jettha " sons shall get two shares ; the remainder is again divided into twenty shares and the " majjhima " daughters shall get one-and-a-half shares ; the remaining property is once more divided into twenty shares and the " majjhima " sons shall get one-and-a-half share. Then divide the property again into twenty shares and give the " kanittha " daughters one share. Of the rest of the property, after being again divided into twenty parts, let the kanittha sons have one share. Then divide the remaining property into ten shares and let the kuddaka daughters have one-and-a-half shares. The property remaining should then be equally divided amongst the eight children.

If the daughter, who is born after the first two children, dies, leaving some children of her own behind, and if the son, who is born after the three " jettha " children, dies (leaving some offspring—E. F.), these orphan children shall receive, if their grandparents are dead, one-fourth of the shares which fall legally to the share of their respective parents.

S. 64. In another way if brothers and sisters, ten in number, are born from the same mother in the following order,—first a son, then two daughters, then a son and daughter, then a son, then two daughters, then a son and then a daughter, they shall be classed as follows :—The son first born and the daughter born next shall be called the *two* eldest ; the three under these the *next* elders. The two sons and the three (daughters), the last daughter being born with a son before her and next to her sister, after the brothers and sisters, three in number, are said to be the youngers. The daughter born last of ten sons and daughters, or last of eight sons and daughters, is called the youngest. After the eldest brother and sister have taken their shares, the remainder shall be divided into two parts over and over again, and the division made as already stated, the remainder shall be divided into two parts and each receive one part.

S. 65. In another way. If sons and daughters, eleven in number, be born from the same mother in the following order,—first four daughters, then two sons, then four daughters, and then a son, they shall be classed as follows :—The first daughter and the second daughter shall be called the *two* eldest, the third and fourth daughters and the fifth born son shall be called the next elders ; the sixth born son, the seventh and eighth sons and daughter shall be called the youngers ; the ninth and the others, in all three, shall be called the three youngest. The division of *property* is similar to the one already stated, but only differs in this one point. After the youngest has received his or her share, *as the case may be*, let the property be divided into fourteen parts, and let the three take three parts, and the remaining eleven parts be equally divided between them all.

S. 66. In another way if sons and daughters, twelve in number, be born from the same mother in the following order,—first four sons, then four daughters, then a son, then a daughter, then a son, and then a daughter, they shall be classed as follows :—The first son, the second son, and the fifth born daughter shall be called the *three* eldest ; the fourth born son, the third born son, and the sixth born daughter shall be called the next elders ; the seventh born daughter, the eighth born daughter, and the ninth born son shall be called the youngers ; the remaining two daughters and the son shall be called the *three* youngest. The division of *property* is similar to the one already stated, but only differs in this point. After the youngest has received his or her share, *as the case may be*, let the property be divided into fifteen parts, and let the three take three parts and the remaining twelve parts be equally divided between them. Other classification of children not yet shown shall be made dependent on the four already stated, and the division of *property* shall also be made as already stated.

S. 67. Moreover the wife has two daughters and the husband has two sons. These two, the widow and widower marry, and two sons only are born to them, after which the widow dies. That step-father then marries one of his wife's daughters, and by her two sons and two daughters are born. On that step-father and dog-like husband dying, the young step-mother marries the husband's son by his first wife (the one before her mother) and begets two daughters and three sons. The young step-mother, who made the son, who was like her nephew, her husband, also dies, and the daughters and sons born in this manner, step by step, amount to fifteen in number, wise men ought to decide the division of the estate (amongst such children) after this manner. The daughters brought by the wife shall take the property which she brought at her marriage. The sons brought by the father shall take the property which he brought at his marriage. The sons by the first marriage of the father and mother receive the property acquired after the marriage. The son born by the father (step) making his step-daughter his wife shall receive the property acquired after the marriage of that husband and wife. In this manner, separating and without causing confusion, each should receive what he is entitled to. Then, dividing into six portions the property of the widow and widower acquired after their marriage, each of the sons originally brought shall receive one portion, the sons by the next step-mother one portion each, and the sons of the same mother and father (နှစ်ပါးရှိသားတို့) shall receive three portions. The (ပါရင်း) property originally brought should be divided into six portions and the after step-mother shall receive one portion and the sons by the after step-mother one portion. The property brought by the step-mother shall be divided into five portions and the first step-father shall receive one portion, the after step-mother four portions. Half the (လက်ထက်ပွား) property acquired after the marriage of the after step-mother shall be given to that step-mother, the other half shall be divided into four portions and the (ပါရင်းအထက်သားတို့) sons originally brought shall receive three portions and the after sons one portion. That step-mother's letthetpwa property shall be divided into four portions, and the former sons shall receive one portion and that step-mother three portions. Some learned men have decided that such should be the division.

S. 68. If a son-in-law buy and sell with his own capital or with that of another person, the capital shall be his property. Then dividing the profits arising from that capital into three portions, the parents-in-law are entitled to two portions and the son-in-law one portion. The reason is because he (son-in-law) lives and eats in his parents-in-law's house. If he trade with the capital of his parents-in-law, the whole belong to the parents-in-law; if the capital belong to the mother and father, the property should be divided into three portions, and the parents-in-law are entitled to one portion.

S. 69. If a son-in-law and daughter live together in the house of the parents-in-law, and if those son-in-law and daughter quarrel, (the parents-in-law) may resume all the property which may have been given to those daughters and sons-in-law. If parents-in-law obtain a son-in-law by purchase, and if the daughter die without issue, that son-in-law when asked shall give the price which was originally given for him. If the property given be still in possession, there is the right to resume the same; if none, there will be no remuneration. If there be sons and grandchildren, the property given in purchasing him shall not be taken back. The profits or increase of the property should be divided into three portions, and the parents-in-law are entitled to one portion and also to the young granddaughter by their daughter.

S. 70. If *parents* after receiving presents from a man give their daughter to him in marriage, and if the daughter die in a separate house, without any issue, the husband alone has a right to all the animate and inanimate property. If she die in her mother and father's house, the mother and father only shall receive and own the whole of the daughter's property, and the husband shall receive and own all the property in the father's house. In other words, whether son or daughter who lives in a separate house comes and dies in the house of his or her mother and father, the whole of the animate and inanimate property belonging to such a one shall be equally divided between the remaining sons and daughters and the mother and father.

S. 71. If a man, without consent, takes by force another person's daughter and lives with her, and if the daughter die without any issue, all the property taken away by the daughter shall be given to the mother alone. The husband has no concern in it. The husband shall alone receive the whole of the animate and inanimate property acquired by good fortune and exertion of both husband and wife. The mother and father have no concern in it.

S. 72. When the son and daughter-in-law and the parents-in-law all live together, and if the *mother* and *father* give them (son and daughter-in-law) capital, and they trade with it, and thereby obtain a large amount of property, and if the wife die before her husband's return, let the capital be the property of the parents-in-law, and let the profits be equally divided into two parts, and let each take one part. If the son-in-law die before his arrival home, it has been shown that the division between the *parents* and the daughter should be similar to *the one above*. The mother and father of the deceased husband shall have no voice *in the matter*.

S. 73. If mother and father with such intentions make over and deposit all the property *with the daughter*, and if that daughter die, the son-in-law shall not alone take all the property thus made over. In the same manner if the father and mother have given the property to the son and if the son die, the daughter-in-law shall not alone take the property. The son-in-law and the parent-in-law, or the daughter-in-law and the parent-in-law, shall divide the property equally between them.

74. If a husband, to escape from care and anxiety, makes over to his wife the charge of all his property, including his slaves, and if his wife in her turn makes over the same to her daughter, and if such daughter dies, her (daughter's) husband shall be the absolute owner of all the said property, and the mother-in-law (or father-in-law) (ေၵာ၁ၵၽၖ) shall be entitled to receive whatever the son-in-law is disposed to bestow on her.

Note (by the author of the *Wonnana*).—*Manu Thara* and other old Dhammathats are somewhat contradictory on this point of law. They say that if a man, wishing to free himself from care and anxiety, makes over to his wife all his animate or inanimate property and if her daughter dies, the son-in-law shall become the absolute master of the property. It is apparent that the wife of the man here spoken of is dead, as the context intends to convey the meaning of the 'mother' rather than the wife.

75. I have hitherto discussed the various points of law when lay people are parties to it, and now my discussion will turn on the subject when ecclesiastics are concerned. If a high priest dies, the maha theras who come next to him shall become absolute owners of his ecclesiastical furniture, his gardens and ponds, and all the religious presents belonging to him. The laythay thera shall receive two shares out of four of all the property and slaves, the laydouk laykhan, who comes next to him in rank, shall receive one share, and the thamane shall receive the remaining share. If there are no laydouk laykhan and the thamanes, their religious associates shall receive the share due to them. The lay pupils shall receive whatever they happen to have in their possession. Although if there is no thamane to inherit the property after the laythay and laydouk theras, their lay pupils and associates shall have no right whatever to any portion of the property besides the one they may happen to have in their possession; as they (the lay pupils) are in no way related to the deceased. The above is a secular law.

76(a). On the death of a high priest, the division of his estate among those who attended him during his illness, the superior laythay thera and other theras and thamanes inferior to him, the lay pupils and the religious associates according to the religious law.

With reference to this point of law, the *Vinaya pitakam* as preached by (Gautama) Buddha enacts as follows :—

During the illness of a high priest, if any one, whether he be the high priest's pupil or a stranger, attends him, the attendant shall be entitled to receive the furniture (parikkhara) used by the deceased priest, his alms-bowl, three of his yellow garments, and also one share of the remaining property. Of the property thus remaining the lay-thay thera shall receive two shares, the thera inferior to him one-and-a-half share, the thamanes one share or half a share.

On the death of the high priest, the laythay thera, who comes next in rank to him, shall receive all the furniture used by the deceased, the gardens and ponds belonging to him, and all the religious gifts received by him. The same superior laythay thera shall again receive two shares out of four into which all the remaining property and slaves are divided. The laykhan thera who may be called the heir (awthara) of the superior laykhan thera, shall receive one share. After these two inheritors have taken their shares, the remaining property shall be divided into four shares, and the pyinzins shall receive three, the thamanes one, the lay pupils being entitled to receive only the property that is in their possession. If there are no surviving pupils of the high priest, the religious associates only are entitled to all the property. If a pupil dies, his teacher shall be entitled to receive the animate and inanimate property of the deceased. If any one attends a sick person (priest ?), he shall receive one share more than his legitimate one.

In the next section I shall proceed to discuss this point more fully according to the *Vinaya pitakam*. I am not prepared to say whether my discussion is correct or not.

(*b*). I empower the religious community to bestow the alms-bowl and the yellow garments of priests on the one who attends a priest in illness. According to the doctrine of our Hpra, one who attends a priest in illness shall get the eight parikkharas, namely, three yellow garments, an alms-bowl, a girdle, a needle, a hatchet, and a water-strainer. The division of the property is allowed as the Hpra decrees that leaving out the garubhan (ဂရုဘ၏) property the remaining lahubhan (လဟုဘ၏) property shall be divided according to the rank of the inheritors in the presence of the community. In support of the truth of the statement the following from the *Mahavagga* may be cited :—

Annjānāmi bhikkhane thapetrāna gavubhandain lahubhadain ratha (zatha ?) vaham samukhibhutma bhajetum.

77. The following 25 articles of property constitute the garubhan property :—
(1) The gardens and (2) lands adjoining to the monastery; (3) the monastery and (4) its site; (5) beds and (6) chairs; (7) mattresses; (8) pillows; (9) brass pots; (10) brass cauldrons; (11) brass cups; (12) brass tubs; (13) files; (14) hatchets; (15) mattocks; (16) large knives (ဓားမ); (17) chisels, (18) canes; (19) bamboos; (20) phyoozan grass (ဖြုဆံမြက်); (21) peit grass (ဗိတ်မြက်); (22) thamanthetkeh grass (သမန်းသက်ငယ်မြက်); (23) white or yellow coloured earths; (24) logs of wood; (25) lands.

The remaining property is called *lahubhan*. The old writers include blank palm-leaves under the head of garubhan. These 25 articles constituting garubhan property are divided under five heads, namely, (1) from the word 'gardens' to the word 'monastery,' (2) from 'beds' to 'pillows,' (3) from 'brass pots' to 'brass cups,' (4) from 'hatchets' to 'chisels,' (5) from 'canes' to 'lands.'

78. If a thera, during his lifetime, gives away his property to another, or it is taken possession of by a friend of his, such property shall devolve upon the receiver or taker of it; and the division of such property shall be according to their will. If no property is given away or taken possession of by any of his friends, but left in any distant place, the priests of that place shall be entitled to claim it, and such priests shall divide it amongst them. The priests who are living in the monastery in which a thera dies shall be entitled to receive all the property which happened to be kept in that monastery. If the inmates of the monastery are living together, the pupils who are present shall get the property. If one of the two priests who are living together dies, the surviving priest shall get all the property of the deceased. In the case of both dying, their property shall devolve upon the religious community, who shall proceed to divide it.

79. The garubhan property shall not at all be divided amongst the religious community or destroyed in any way, whether the priests from the four quarters be present or not. The pupils who are living in the same monastery may divide the lahubhan property amongst themselves. When there are no such pupils, all the property shall

devolve upon the religious community. Even if all such property be dedicated property, the religious community shall bestow the eight kinds of furniture (parikkhara) on the person—even if such person were a woman—who attended the deceased during his illness.

80. On the death of a thamane his property shall be similarly divided. The foregoing laws hold good in all the divisions of estates belonging to the priesthood. If all the Vinaya laws bearing on the subject be here reproduced, this work would be swelled. Therefore I have made only relevant extracts and references for the right understanding of the law and which, I hope, would be borne in mind by legislators. Thinking the Dhammathats of old do not agree with the Holy Scriptures on such points I have undertaken to convey them. I hope all learned men by the light of their wisdom will repel the darkness which is over the face of the laws.

S. 81. If a rahan die and his property be the offerings made by others (strangers), his relations and the members of his family should not get his property. The disciples and those who *attended on him during his illness* only are entitled to it. If the property had been given to the rahan by his parents, his disciples and fellow-rahans are not entitled to it, but his relations only are entitled : the reason is because the property belongs not to the priesthood. If a rahan, by cultivation, trading, or usury, acquire property in abundance, his mother and father and members of his family are entitled to it.

Another mode is, if a rahan by usury acquire property and he die, the "peesin" priest should receive two portions of it, the "thamanay" one portion, and the mother and father and relatives half a portion. Thus should the property be divided and taken : the reason is because if any punishment be ordered by the ruler *on the rahan*, the parents and relations and those of the house shall bear it.

S. 82. If a layman offer an individual rahan a garden, paddy land, cows, buffaloes, carriage, cart, slave, robe, vessels to receive offerings of food, kyoung, or cups and other vessels, on the death of the priest the layman who made the offerings is entitled to all the goods. If such offerings be made for the use of the priesthood generally, the priesthood only is then entitled to it. Thus it is commonly written regarding offerings made to the priesthood generally. This old writing should be considered.

S. 83. If a Brahmin die and has disciples and members of his family (alive), these disciples and members of his family only are entitled to the whole of his property. If he have none, the Brahmins who live with him and have a clear conscience (သုခတဘကြည်ဖြောသာ) are entitled to it. But if there is no (such) fellow-Brahmins, the king ruling the country is entitled to it. If there be no such heirs, the king is entitled to the property of the rahan and Brahmin. So said teachers of old.

Note.—See 8 Moore's Indian appeals 500.

CHAPTER II.

THE LAW REGARDING SONS.

S. 84. There are six different classes of sons, which are these: awratha son, hettima son, pokepaga son, kittima son, and appadita son. There are also six different classes of sons, which are called dainaka son, thahooda son, poonanodebawa son, kaiteta son, thuanotta son, and sahtabattee son. The lastmentioned six classes of sons are only called sons, but they have no right to inherit their parents' property, or, in other words, the said two six different classes of. sons are called sons and therefore have a link to the inheritance. The former mode was based on the six classes *of sons*, and excellent and enquiring teachers made use of that common mode.

> *Note.*—According to the Hindu writers there are 12 kinds of sons, six of whom are heirs, the other six not. The Hindu classifications have evidently something to do with those of the Burmese Codes, *e.g.*, awratha: aurasa; thahooda: sahodha; poonanodebawa: paunarbhava; pathawtaka, or patha as the *Menu Kyay* calls him: parasava; kiethiema: kritima; while apatitha or appadita resembles apavidha and khetadza khsetraja. , A proper philological research would propably show more borrowing of the same kind. But the definitions in the Hindu and Burmese books do not always correspond. Even in India from the earliest times the priority of different sons varied with the prevalent opinions: the process is displayed in the Tagore lectures, 1880, and the reader may consult Colebrooke. In the papers about wills, an elder of Shwaygyin writes as if there were six castes among Burmans, and adds that each of these have six classes of sons, as if this part of the code were in full operation. In India the Judges have disinherited most of them and treated the old law as abrogated now; the properly adopted son alone among the eleven secondary sons can inherit in this kali yug.

S. 85. Of the sons above mentioned, the firstmentioned six classes of sons are entitled to inherit their parents' property, and the sons lastmentioned are only entitled to get what is given to them.

S. 86. There are also sixteen classes of sons, which are these: awratha son, wieneewathookee son, whom excellent teachers call winiwathookyain son, khettadza son, parawiethookee son, meggahtawa son, moohtala son, karanee son, thahahtaka son, kareebhatta son, dhanoobhawa son, thwazata son, pathawtaka son, wottara son, pamootta son, antewathieka son, and deinnaka son.

S. 87. Out of the sixteen kinds of sons, the awratha son is the son of mother and father given in marriage by mutual consent and the consent of the parents of both.

S. 88. Both the mother and father consent to the marriage, but should a son be born before the marriage, such a one is called a weineewathookee son.

S. 89. Both the mother and father consent to the marriage, but the daughter not approving of the man takes another and begets a son by him, such a son is called a khettadza son. Former teachers have said that khettadza son is the son of a slave woman; on taking into consideration the opinion is that it is improper.

S. 90. Both the mother and father do not agree, but the son and the daughter (girl) by mutual consent live together and get a son, such a son is called a parawiethookee son.

S. 91. When a person has been turned out of the family and relations and that persons gets a son in another place, such a son is called a meggahtawa son.

S. 92. *Persons* given in marriage by mutual consent get a son before the proper time (seven or nine months), such a son is called a moohtala son.

S. 93. The son born of a *woman* without a husband is called a karanee son or a thahahtaka son.

S. 94. The son of a slave woman bought with money is called a kareebhatta son.

S. 95. The husband not loving the wife turns her out, she returns to *him* pregnant by another and bears a son, such a son is called a dhanoobhawa son.

S. 96. A son turned out by the mother and father from amongst his relations for his bad habits is called a thwazata son.

S. 97. The son of a Brahmin father by a woman not a Brahminee is called a pathawtaka son.

S. 98. The son whose father is unknown is called a wottara son.

S. 99. If a man lives and *has sexual connection* (ကြိုလာ့ဦးနှုတ်ရှိတော်) with the *girl* aimed at for his wife and thereby begets a son, such a son is called a pamootta son.

S. 100. A son dependent on teachers with an aim to acquire knowledge (gain education) is called an antewathieka son.

S. 101. A son given by others is called a deinnaka son, in other words, the son given away to others is called a deinnaka son. Thus the sons are divided into sixteen classes.

S. 102. The awratha sons shall inherit the property of their parents before the other sixteen kinds of sons. The other sons have no right whatever to any property other than that which their father has given into their hands. If they have obtained, through the favour of their parents, some property, they have no legal right to its possession; if, however, on the death of the parents the elder brothers (phâtu) give them some property, they have a right to keep it. The claim to property by the many kinds of heirs notwithstanding, the parents, who are masters over (the heirs), have an absolute right over their property; any property given away by the parents may be legally retained. [So far the Pali text; the author of the *Wonnana* adds in Burmese the following remarks :—Many commentators have explained " tesam " in the passage contained in the second gatha, "tesam satisa samike," as the law obtaining between the parents and children. As this is a chapter on " inheritance" and not on the " rights of slaves," I believe " tesam " is not to be interpreted as " lord," which the context suggests. I understand this passage as meaning that " before parents have died or separated, no heirs, however legiti-" mate their claims may be, shall have any right whatever to demand " the division of an estate, or to keep any portion of it as their irrevo-" cable possession, but that they have a right to retain what has been " given into their possession." The reader is left to exercise his discretion on this point. The word " samika " not only means " lord," but, according to the grammar, also " husband." If the text refers to the "lord of the parents" the interpretation should be according to the context.]

Note.—As the above law does not treat of the relation of slaves to their lord, but of the rights of parents over their property, it is to be taken in the sense of "masters" over their property against the claims of the different kinds of heirs. —E. F.

S. 103. A son who does not take the instructions of the mother and father (or who is disobedient) is not entitled to the estate of the mother and father; the parents only have the right. In accordance with "Tsadotehtapota" when the mother is dead, although such a son ask the father, he should not get any portion. When the father is dead, although *that son* ask the mother, he should not get any portion. The living father or mother *as the case may be* is alone entitled. If that son steal anything from his mother and father, he should receive the punishment for theft, because he has broken the law of the duties of a son.

Note.—See the following decisions of Mr. Sandford as to rights of children in his rulings:—Adopted child living separately, p. 4; evidence of adoption, p. 22; right of illegitimate child to inherit in default of others, p. 11; child of first marriage, p. 14; the publicly adopted child has some rights as a natural child, p. 30.

S. 104. Of two sons, one of whom is born before marriage and the other born after marriage, the son born after marriage is at the death of the mother and father the inheritor. The one born before marriage is not an heir.

S. 105. Of two sons, one born while the person (father) is a rahan and the other when he had left the priesthood (turned a layman), which must be regarded as awratha or legitimate son? Those sons born after (he had left the priesthood) only are to be regarded (as legitimate) as awratha.

S. 209. If *the man*, for the benefit of *both* man and wife, is anxious to go to a distant place, he should leave means of subsistence for his wife and then go. If he goes away without thus leaving, and his wife from poverty borrows from another and makes use of the same, and being unable to pay *her* debts, the creditor cohabits (ပေါယာဥ်ပါ) with that man's wife and openly takes her for his own wife, the husband should not say that the creditor ought to pay damage.

Note.—In III Notes on Buddhist law the Indian opinion is pointed out.

S. 210. Debts incurred by former wives shall not be demanded from new (after) wives. Debts incurred by new (after) wives shall not likewise be demanded from former wives. Debts incurred by former husbands shall not be demanded from new (after) husbands, and debts incurred by new (after) husbands shall not likewise be demanded from former husbands. If, when asked from the remaining wives to the knowing and seeing of that husband and wife, it be said that *the debt* would be given, there is the right to ask for all such debts *from that husband and wife.*

S. 258(*a*). A *person* dying who has in the possession of others property in expectancy, bribes that have been given, property entrusted, and property pledged, the heirs have the right to claim all such property ; others have not the right to claim.

(*b*). If the person die having the property in expectancy, bribes that have been given, property entrusted and property pledged, in his possession, the heirs should give up such property. If there be such property, it should not be included in inheritance property and taken. Even if the property be such, if there is no knowledge of it being so, it should not be given. Thus it should be shown.

S. 259. A debtor dies and his corpse is buried. If it be the village loogyee *who buries*, there is no fault. If it be a friend, he should pay one-fourth of the debts. If it be a relative, he should pay one-third *of the debts*. If the heirs bury *the corpse*, all the debts which should be paid should be paid *by them*.

Note.—See the *Menu Kyay*, Bk. 10, ss. 62 and 63 ; and for a judicial interpretation, Nga Tsan Yoon's case at p. 45 of Sandford's Rulings.

S. 260. If mother and father give to their kittima son property to be used as capital and then give him in marriage (ⲟⲟ⳿ⲟⲟⳅ), that kittima son then gains during the lifetime of the mother and father. On the death of the mother and father that kittima son shall pay all debts. If there be the awratha son who is an inheritor, that own (legitimate) son alone shall pay all debts.

S. 423. Of buying and selling there are four kinds : One is selling when the price is decided in the presence of arbitrators ; one is selling in the absence of those who know and see and of arbitrators ; one is buying when the price is decided in the presence of other arbitrators ; one is buying in the absence of those who know and see and of arbitrators. Thus wise men have shown that there are two and two kinds of buying and selling (two of buying and two of selling).

S. 424. Goods that are in a distant place ; goods that dared not be shown to arbitrators ; goods that are of no value ; goods that are known to be unsound ; these are the four kinds of goods that ought not to be bought. If these four kinds of goods be bought, a mistake will be made.

Note.—As pointed out in **IV** Notes on Buddhist law; the doctrine about purchases in good faith is similar in the Burmese Codes and such Indian Codes as the *Vyavahara Mayukha*. For the ancient texts from which much of Book 2 of the *Menu Kyay* and chapter 7 of the *Vyavahara* are made up, see Colebrook's Digest on sale without ownership.

S. 454. If purchase of garden or paddy land be made, after valuing the same, and if, before *any plants* have been planted, the seller again sells it to others, he shall pay two for one (*i.e.*, double). If that value is not demanded, for, for some reason or other, *the land* was not worked or *plants* planted, it may be worked when the rains are plentiful.

S. 455. If a person accepts a mortgage of redeemable land, the price of the land shall again be given on the expiration of three years. If this has not been given, and five years or five seedtimes have passed, then half the price of the land shall be obtained.

If this has not been given after five years or five seedtimes, and ten years or ten seedtimes have passed, that land shall be given to its owner. As *the person* has for ten years continually worked and enjoyed the produce of the land, *he* should as an honest person return the land to its owner. Thus the meaning is known.

S. 456. Whether the mode given before be suitable or not, I shall again show another mode. When toddy, betelnut, and such like trees be sold, mortgaged, or bought, if that which is worth 100 be bought for 50, this mortgaging for half price is called " poung-shin" (living mortgage, hence redeemable). When the owners of the trees wish to redeem (their trees), they shall only on payment of the amount for which they were mortgaged receive back their trees. Though such mortgage should be made, yet the person through poverty mortgages for half of 50, and if it be said that the other half would be given once in every three years (by instalments), and according to the saying, if after every three years *some portion* of the price be given out of the balance half, and the trees worked (fruits plucked), the original owner can only get back the trees on payment of the amount for which they were mortgaged. If after the completion of three years their *price* be not given, and if the trees be worked (used) for three years and the produce enjoyed, though the amount for which mortgaged be not given, the original owners only are entitled to take *back* all those toddy, cocoanut, betelnut, and such like trees. This kind of mortgaging and selling is called " kyapoung;" the enjoyment of the fruits is *equivalent* to the labour and the value (amount for which mortgaged). If through regard *a thing* worth 100 is accepted in mortgage for 100 and the person who sold or mortgaged did so by saying that if he wished to redeem the same he would do so by paying the amount for which it was mortgaged, and if the purchaser or (mortgagee) agree to these terms, and if the owner wish to redeem that property, he should pay the amount for which it was mortgaged and then take the same. If *that amount be* not given, that owner shall not get. This kind of mortgaging and selling is called " thwinpoung."

S. 457(*a*). In other words, wise men ought to divide sale and purchase into three classes, viz., ahpine (အဖိုး), apoungh (အပေါင်), and tinpoung (တင်ပေါင်), or kyapoung (ကျပေါင်).

(*b*). If a *thing* worth one hundred *tickals* is sold or mortgaged for one hundred *tickals*, it is called ahpine ; if it is sold or mortgaged for fifty, it is called ahpoung ; if it is sold for the half of fifty, it is called tinpoung or kyapoung.

(*c*). If *the produce* of a paddy land which would yield one hundred baskets of paddy is enjoyed, *that land* is worth sixty *tickals*. If *that land* be bought for sixty tickals, it is called ahpine. If it is bought for thirty, it is called ahpoung.

(*d*). If only fifteen tickals be given, it is called tinpoung. After every three years of that tinpoung the value should be filled (give till completion): all the remaining (other property) should *be decided* according to the modes abovementioned.

5

S. 458(*a*). If seller and buyer sell and buy a piece of land as "myatheh" (outright) and if one of them (seller or buyer) die, and if there be heirs of that deceased, there is the right for the *land* to be redeemed or given, if thus be the wish. If both of them (buyer or seller) be not dead (both living), *the* land cannot be redeemed though there be such a desire. This mode of selling, mortgaging, and buying is called "myatheh."

(*b*). In another way, if, during the lifetime of heirs, sale and purchase be effected by mother and father against the will of heirs, and if after the land shall have come to the possession of others and after the death of the mother and father these daughters and sons who are heirs are desirous of redeeming the land, that land is redeemable land (they shall have the right to do so); but if the sale and purchase shall have been made with the consent and knowledge and in the presence of the *heirs* though their own mother and father shall die, yet that land is not redeemable, (the heirs) shall not have the right to redeem.

(*c*). If the sons and grandchildren of the buyer be desirous of selling the land, they should sell it to the sons and grandchildren of the original owner of the land; but if the (latter) be unwilling to buy the land, then the former shall sell the land to others as they like.

Note.—For judicial construction of this section and of s. 1, Bk. 8, of the *Menu Kyay*, see pages 37 and 40 of Rulings by Sandford J.

S. 459. All kinds of sale and purchase should not be made when in stocks or in irons, *i.e.*, when the person is in custody; and if such, it cannot be called sale or purchase. If an action (အမှု) is authoritatively and forcibly ordered to be done, such is not called an action. If property be snatched and taken, twice its *value* should be paid and the person should be punished (မင်းဒါဏ်). Thus it should be shown. Wise men ought not to buy slaves and property of the person in difficulties. It is wrong if they buy. Though sale and purchase be made, it ought not to be called sale and purchase.

S. 472(*a*). Revenue on lands given by men of old for sacred purposes shall not on any account be destroyed (used), in other words, lands given for sacred purposes by ruling kings shall not be destroyed by any person. The mean and wicked person who destroys shall after death go to hell for ever. Even during the lifetime of *such a person*, his bodily ease, comfort, and fame shall decrease. Lands dedicated to sacred purposes shall not be destroyed even as much as a cubit, a span, the breadth of a finger, or half a hair's breadth (hence not at all). Thus wise men of old have pointed out.

(*b*). During the time of our venerable Phra (Gautama) King Pahthanadee Kawthalah (မဂ္ဂင်ဘောင်—) took a thousand presents (ပဏ္ဍာဋ္ဌင်) from heretics and gave them (heretics) a piece of land for a kyoung near Zaidahwoon kyoung. The excellent Phra who conveys *persons to neikban* in a magic raft (ပသေနဒီကောသလ) hearing what had happened, ordered, saying that it (the giving of the land to the heretics) was not proper. After having thus ordered, the excellent Phra related former affairs, saying, " Oh King, during " my time and previous, King Goororit ruled over the country of " Goororit, and on the northern side of that country (Goororit) there " was a tree covered only with branches. Once upon a time two rathais " (hermits), who were rulers of two gines (classes of pupils) and who " were endowed with supernatural powers, came from Haimawoonto " forests and lived in (under) that tree. A quarrel arose between them " from a dispute as to the ownership of the tree, and they (rathais) " petitioned to the King of the country.   The King, oh King " *Pathanadee Kawthalah,* on hearing that the embryo Phra was the one " who first arrived at the country, decided that the rathai who first " arrived at the country shall get the tree.   The raithai who came " afterwards (to the country) then offered the carriage-box used by Tsat " Kya Min.   On receiving the carriage-box the King decided again " that the two rathais shall share equally (the tree).   Oh King " *Pathanadee Kawthalah,* the rathai who was your embryo Phra then " offered the wheels of the carriage of Tsat Kya Min.   On receiving " them the King again decided that the rathai who first arrived shall " receive it (tree).   Having known the facts regarding King Goororit, " the excellent rathai and his 500 followers possessed with supernatural " powers returned to Haimawoonta forests.   After this the Nats who " watch over the country being angry covered the Goororit country, " which in area is three ' yohzanahs,' with the waters of the great " ocean.   The waters of the ocean destroyed the whole country."   As the old story goes to show that for the sake of one king all the people were destroyed, cases for lands and waters should be well enquir- ed into and decided.

   Note.—Sakkya Meng, *i.e.,* the King Cakra, is the ruler of the Tavattimsa heaven on the top of Mount Meru.

Translation of the Law of Inheritance according to the Wagaru Dhammathat by Dr. E. Forchhammer, Professor of Pali, from a Pali Manuscript on Palm Leaves in his possession.

NOTE.—Since I sent to the Press the annotated translation of the Burmese *Wonnana* on inheritance I have been favoured by Dr. E. Forchhammer with this translation of the Pali manuscript of the *Wagaru* Dhammathat on the same subject. Aware of its high importance to learning I lose no time in printing it. For some account of the *Wagaru* the reader is referred to what Dr. Forchhammer has written in III and IV Notes on Buddhist law: "At the close of the 15th and the " beginning of the 16th centuries a Talaing thero, Budhaghosha, acquired great fame " as a jurist: he was called to the courts of Pugan and the King of Siam to settle " difficult law disputes. With him begins the authenticated history of Burmese " Dhammathats. I have found a copy of the, probably, most ancient version of the " *Manoo Sara* extant. Budhaghosha translated it, as he himself expressly states, " from the original Talaing into Pali and Burmese:—' I, the TheroBudhaghosha, de-" sirous of promoting the interest of religion, translated faithfully (according to the " letter) the *Wagaru* Dhammathat, written in the Talaing language.' The Talaing " version, he further states, was arranged by Wagaru (Wah-ra-roo), a King of Marta-" ban, who began his reign in the year 1280 A.D."

The *Wagaru* bears distinct traces of Hindu origin; and as the *Wonnana* is based upon it, the scholar will be able to identify those parts of the latter code, which are accretions to that used by the Talaings. It is to be hoped that the changes effected during the intervening centuries will be elucidated by a careful comparison of the other Dhammathats. It is possible that recent additions may have been made from the Hindu law books; and it appears certain that customs of the Burmán people were incorporated and given force of law.—J. Jardine.

O GREAT king, the following is the law of inheritance :—Division of inherited property may be effected (1) among sons on the death of their father ; (2) among daughters and their father on the death of their mother ; (3) among sons and daughters on the death of their parents ; (4) among children and their step-mother on the death of their father ; (5) among children and their step-father on the death of their mother ; (6) among former and later children (*i. e.*, born of different mothers or fathers) ; (7) among step-sons and their half-brothers. Thus the Lord Manu has decided.

2. Oh great king, on the death of a father his awratha (orasa) son shall get the personal property (paribhoga) of his father, his cups, knives, ornaments, slaves utilized and fed by his father, and his elephants, horses, oxen, and buffaloes. Of the remaining property of the father, the mother shall receive three-fourths, and the remaining one-fourth share shall be divided amongst the awratha son and the other sons. The division of this one share is as follows :—It shall be divided into ten shares and the awratha son shall get two ; the remaining property shall again be divided into ten shares and the eldest daughter shall get two ; the remainder is again divided into ten portions and the younger son (the one next to the awratha) shall receive one ; dividing the remaining portion again into ten shares the younger daughter shall receive one. The remaining property is again divided into ten portions and the youngest son shall receive one share

and a half; the remaining property shall be again divided into ten shares and the youngest daughter shall receive one share and a half. If any property remains after such division, it shall be equally divided amongst the children. Thus has the Lord Manu decreed the division of property to be.

3. Oh great king, on the death of the mother the awratha daughter (orasadhita) shall receive the gold ornaments used by, and belonging to, her mother; the female slaves of her mother also fall to her share. Of the remaining property the father shall receive three-fourths, and the remaining one-fourth share shall be divided between the eldest daughter and the rest of the family in the same manner as shown in the preceding paragraph.

4. Oh great king, on the death of both parents the eldest son shall receive the personal property of the father and the eldest daughter the personal property of the mother; of the remaining property the eldest son shall receive two shares, the younger son one share, and the younger daughter one-third of a share; if the younger daughter is older than the younger son, both of them shall get equal shares; the younger (middle, majjhima) son and younger daughter shall obtain equal shares, and so also the youngest sons and youngest daughters.

Thus decided the Lord Rishi Manu.

5. Oh great king, if the father dies and the mother takes a second husband, this second husband shall receive after his wife died one-fifth of the original property (ပါရင်းဥစ္စာ) and five-sevenths of the increased (letthetpwa) property; the step-children shall get the remaining two-sevenths.

6. If on the death of the mother, the father, after having taken a second wife, dies, the second wife shall divide the property in the same manner as set forth in the preceding case. Thus Manu has decided.

7. Oh great King, the division of property among former sons (pubbaputta, sons of the former marriage) is thus : the sons of a former husband (pubbapatikaputta) shall receive the original property (လင်ကြီးကပါရင်းဥစ္စာ) of their father; and the sons of the former wife (pubbakamataputta) shall receive the original property of their mother. The step-father or the step-mother shall then divide the increased (letthetpwa) property into four shares, and give two shares to the former sons (of a former marriage) and two shares to the sons born after the (present) marriage. If there has been no increase of property after the marriage, the original property shall be divided into five shares and the sons born after the marriage (နှစ်ပါးဖြစ်ေ သာသားတို့) shall get one share. If no sons are born after the marriage, let the property be equally divided among the former sons of the father or the mother.

Thus Manu has decided.

8. Oh great king, if property is to be divided among one's own children (thus the Burmese text; the Pali gives orasaputta, E. F.) and adopted children (kittima) of a husband or wife, and provided they live together with their parents, the awratha sons shall receive

five-sixths and the adopted children the remaining one-sixth of the property. If, however, the adopted children do not live under the roof of their adopters, they shall forfeit their share of inheritance.

9. If there are no awrathas, the property shall be divided amongst the adopted children and the relatives of the deceased. If there are neither awrathas (the Pali *orasa* has two distinct meanings,—first, it means the eldest of one's own children ; and, secondly, one's own or legitimate children collectively as opposed to adopted children—E. F.) nor adopted children nor any relatives, the property falls under the jurisdiction of the king (raja danda bhavati ; the Burmese translation says " it shall become the king's property "—E. F.).

Thus Manu has decided.

10. Oh great king, if an estate is to be divided among the three kinds of sons, the awratha (orasa) sons shall receive four shares, the younger (hettima, *i. e.*, the lower sons, or probably those of a lower wife—E. F.) one share, and the sons born of a female slave (khettajā) half a share. If the female slave is still living, her sons shall receive as their inheritance the price of their own mother's body.

Thus Manu has decided.

11. Oh great king, the Lord Manu has decided that the property of a man should be thus divided among the four kinds of wives :—If one of them belongs to the royal family (raja kula), she shall receive one share out of four ; if she belongs to a Brahman family (Brahmana kula), she receives three shares ; if she is of the class of merchants (vanija kula), she receives two shares ; and if she belongs to the cultivators (khetta kula), one share.

The sons of such wives are entitled to the inheritance in the same proportion as their respective mothers.

Thus Manu has decided.

12. Oh great king, if in a family a child is born of defective or equivocal sex, that child is not entitled to an equal share of the inheritance with the other co-heirs ; only so much should be given to them that they can live. (The Pali text implies that they have no right to any share in the inheritance—dayajjamnakhadeyya—beyond that their food should be given to them—bhunjitam dhanam dadeyya.—E. F.) If such children live with their parents, but do not assist them in their work and attend to their wants, they shall forfeit even that claim to inheritance (*i. e.*, of having the bare means of subsistence given to them).

13. If there are married elder daughters and a married younger (hettima) son, the eldest daughter and this son shall enjoy the estate of their parents. If, however, a daughter brings forth children by a man who has not received the consent of the parents to marry their daughter, such children have no claim whatever to their grandparents' property.

Thus has Manu decided.

14. Oh great king, there are twelve kinds of sons, of which six are entitled to inherit the property of their parents and six are not entitled. The first six are the *awratha putto* (orasa putto, either in the sense of the eldest son or of a legitimate son) ; the *hettima putto* (either in the sense of a younger son or a son by a lower wife) ; the

khettajā (a son born by a female slave) ; the *pubbaka putto* (or the son of a former marriage) ; the *kittima putto* (or the publicly adopted son) ; and the *apatittha putto* (the homeless boy, who has no protection, whose parents and relatives are unknown or dead). The following six kinds of sons are not entitled to inherit the property of their deceased parents : (1) sons given by others ; (2) sons bought with money ; (3) a son born by one's wife, but begotten by another man ; (4) a son begotten in indiscreet amorous play (by young unmarried people?) ; (5) "dog sons," that is, such sons as defy the authority of their parents and lead a vagabond life ; (6) poor, hunger-stricken children, who are fed and brought up.

Thus the Lord Rishi Manu has decided.